Dear Reader:

The book you are about to [read is] St. Martin's True Crime L[ibrary, which the New York] Times calls "the leader in tr[ue crime. We offer] you a fascinating account of [the latest, most sensational crime] that has captured the nation[al attention. St. M]artin's is the publisher of perennial bestselling true crime author Jack Olsen (SON and DOC) whose SALT OF THE EARTH is the true story of how one woman fought and triumphed over life-shattering violence; Joseph Wambaugh called it "powerful and absorbing." DEATH OF A LITTLE PRINCESS recounts the investigation into the horrifying murder of child beauty queen JonBenét Ramsey. FALLEN HERO is the *New York Times* bestselling account of the O.J. Simpson case. Peter Meyer tells how a teenage love pact turned deadly in BLIND LOVE: *The True Story of the Texas Cadet Murders*. For those who believe slavery is a thing of the past, Wensley Clarkson proves them wrong in SLAVE GIRLS: *The Shocking World of Human Bondage*. Fannie Weinstein and Melinda Wilson tell the story of a beautiful honors student who was lured into the dark world of sex for hire in THE COED CALL GIRL MURDER.

St. Martin's True Crime Library gives you the stories *behind* the headlines. Our authors take you right to the scene of the crime and into the minds of the most notorious murderers to show you what really makes them tick. St. Martin's True Crime Library paperbacks are better than the most terrifying thriller, because it's all true! The next time you want a crackling good read, make sure it's got the St. Martin's True Crime Library logo on the spine—you'll be up all night!

Charles E. Spicer, Jr.
Senior Editor, St. Martin's True Crime Library

WHO IS JACK BARRON?

- **ABANDONED CHILD?** Jack Barron had always been obsessed with thoughts of his absent father, a railroad engineer who left the family when Jack was a teenager

- **"MAMA'S BOY"?** Roberta Barron seems to have coddled her son from a young age, turning him into a demanding, indulged child with serious behavior problems

- **MANIPULATIVE PSYCHOPATH?** Jack Barron's daily adult behavior was characterized by an excessive concern with how others viewed him, continuously blaming others for his own failures, and using the deaths of his family members to gain sympathy from outsiders

- **DELUSIONAL LADIES' MAN?** After the death of his wife, country singer Wynonna Judd extended her sympathies to Barron and invited him and his daughter to two concerts. Barron told neighbors that he and the singer were secretly dating

OR *WORSE*?

FIND OUT MORE ABOUT THE MAN
ACCUSED OF SMOTHERING
TO DEATH HIS WIFE AND CHILDREN . . .

St. Martin's Paperbacks True Crime Library titles by Carlton Smith

DYING *for* DADDY

CARLTON SMITH

St. Martin's Paperbacks

DYING FOR DADDY

Cover photograph by Olan Mills.

ISBN: 0-312-96632-6

Printed in the United States of America

St. Martin's Paperbacks edition / August 1998

St. Martin's Paperbacks are published by St. Martin's Press, 175 Fifth Avenue, New York, N.Y. 10010.

10 9 8 7 6 5 4 3 2 1

I am really sorry you're unhappy right now. I have a hard time believing the only reason for this is my inability to keep the house exactly the way you like it. . . . We usually have so much fun together. We have so much to be happy and thankful for . . . It really upsets me when I hear you talk about divorce . . . Things have been so good for us for so long, you don't just wake up one day and suddenly decide something like that.

> *All my love,*
> *Irene*

—from the Warrant for the Arrest of Jack Kenneth Barron

Author's Note and Acknowledgments

One by one, over a period of 32 months, the members of Jack Barron's family died. First his wife, Irene, was found dead in her bed; then his four-year-old son, Jeremy, was found dead in his bed; then his four-year-old daughter, Ashley, was found dead in her bed; and finally, Jack Barron's mother was found dead—in her bed, as well.

Authorities in Sacramento, California at first believed they were confronted with a medical mystery of astounding dimensions: how could three members of the same family die of apparently unknown natural causes? But when Jack Barron's mother, Roberta Butler, was found dead at the end of February, 1995, the authorities came to the conclusion that it wasn't illness that killed the Barrons, but something infinitely more sinister—murder.

This is the story of Jack Barron, and the deaths that seemed to haunt him, and which were eventually to result in his being charged, in a most unusual case, as being a serial killer of his own family.

Drawn from court records, coroners' reports, a video-taped interrogation of Jack Barron, and interviews with more than 40 individuals familiar with the bizarre case, the Barron family deaths continue to pose a series of puzzles.

Why, for example, did it take authorities in Sacramento so long to decide that three deaths were, in fact, a case of serial murder? And, if the authorities had acted sooner, might three people still be alive today?

Those are questions that this book proposes to answer, while providing a close look at the sort of circumstances that may seem perfectly ordinary from the outside, but might have been conditions for the most heinous of crimes.

A word about quotes in this book: in cases where the actual words spoken were unavailable, but the gist of the conversation was recalled or otherwise accessible, the conversation is paraphrased without quote marks. In all other cases, where quote marks are employed, it is because the actual words were available, either on tape or as reconstructed by the participants.

During the period in which this book was assembled, the author enjoyed the generous cooperation of a number of individuals. Primary among them were John Paget, brother of Irene Barron; Irene Barron's best friend, Denise Call, and her husband Cliff; the staff of Sacramento County Coroner Bill Brown, including Supervising Coroner Bob Bowers, Coroner's Deputy Billy Guillot, and forensic pathologist Dr. Gregory Reiber; Sacramento Sheriff's Detective Maryl Lee Cranford; Sacramento Deputy District Attorney John O'Mara; Assistant Public Defender Donald Manning; Benicia, California, police officers Monty Castillo, Tom Dalby and Lt. Mike Daley; and Solano County Deputy District Attorney Chris Pedersen and DA's investigator Al Garza. My grateful thanks to everyone for their patience and their help.

Carlton Smith
San Francisco, California
1997

BENICIA, CALIFORNIA
Monday, February 27, 1995

One

Punchout time came sooner than Jack expected, almost before he was ready. He'd risen before dawn—what was it, 4:30 A.M.?—to drive to his new job on the trains. Even though he was sick, Jack wanted to show his new bosses they could depend on him.

For the first time in many years, Jack had all the reasons he needed to be happy. It was the new job. After years of shelving canned goods, paper products, and cereal boxes, of being a rarely noticed grunt worker in the anonymous aisles of supermarkets from Shasta to Sacramento, Jack finally had a real job, the one he'd always wanted: he was a railroad man.

The thundering throb of the locomotives, loud enough to make the air vibrate and the ground shake with all the power they contained, had always thrilled Jack Barron. The sheer, frightening energy of the gigantic diesel engines, the whoosh of the air hoses, the squeal of the braking wheels on the hard steel of the tracks, coupled with the intense awareness that a single moment's inattention could result in instant annihilation, all bespoke the awesome magic of the world of rails.

The world of trains had been important to Jack almost

as long as he could remember. It had begun when he was small, when his father was an engineer for the Southern Pacific. Being able to control the enormous power of the locomotive, the complex switching mechanisms, the time and motion and distance of the elaborate network that tied a continent into a steel-solid whole—this was satisfaction the ordinary man might never enjoy. From the cab of a locomotive, the whistle said it all, even if the pay was only $13 an hour and change.

Not that Jack got to go very far, at least so far; he hadn't seen much of America yet. As a new hire for Amtrak's Northern California operations, Jack was the low man on the signal-pole; although grandly titled Assistant Conductor, Jack spent most of his time helping two other men assemble the Amtrak trains at the Alameda, California, maintenance yard—hooking up the airbrake hoses between the locomotives and the passenger cars, relaying hand signals between the conductor at the rear of the train and the engineer in front, and in general, helping to bring this newly composed train into the Oakland depot, where the operating crew would take over, after which the passengers to points north, south, and east would take their seats.

After that, for Jack and his co-workers, it was back to the maintenance yard to put another train away, and to get yet another train together for the journey into the heartland of America. Grunt work, it was.

But still, it was railroad work, just as he'd yearned for, for almost 20 years—ever since the day in the early 1970s when his father, Elmore the railroad engineer, had walked out of Jack's life and had never come back, thereby leaving a 13-year-old boy to wonder what it was that he had to do to be a man.

Jack had wanted this railroad job so badly for so long that his mother Roberta, despite her bitterness toward Elmore, had prayed every night, rosary in hand, for Jack to get his wish, his chance on the Big Steel.

On this Monday, February 27, Jack spent his worktime

with Frank Klatt, the conductor, and Phil Gosney, the engineer. Together the trio worked to retrieve locomotives from the roundhouse, connect them to the cleaned and serviced passenger cars, and run the assembled train into the Oakland station five minutes away.

Then, as usual, the three would wait for an incoming train, pick up that train when it arrived, and deliver it back to the yard, where the locomotive and the cars would be separated, the engine washed down, and the cars delivered for servicing. Jack spent much of the time with either Klatt at the rear of the train, with Gosney in the cab, or in between the two as Jack connected the cars or relayed hand signals from Klatt to Gosney, or from Gosney to Klatt. It was fairly intense work: a lot of running around, punctuated by intermittent periods of inactivity while the crew waited for another train to arrive or depart.

But just after 1:30 P.M., the workday was over. Klatt and Gosney marched to the timeclock at the stationhouse and punched out promptly. So did Jack.

As he drove his van east on State Highway 24, through the Caldecott Tunnel burrowed under the Berkeley hills, through the suburb of Lafayette and down into Walnut Creek, Jack considered his relationship with his mother, Roberta. They'd had a few troubles recently—pretty much what you might expect when a 34-year-old man moves back home to share space with his 52-year-old parent.

She still treats me like I'm 13 or 14 sometimes, Jack thought. It was irritating.

But, Jack supposed, occasional flare-ups were only to be expected under the circumstances. Roberta Butler had never been known as any kind of shrinking violet when expressing her opinions. She had a tart tongue and was quick to use it. Still, he loved his mom, and he was sure she loved him. After all, she'd stood by him, no matter how bad it had gotten over the past few years, even when people had said things that weren't fair . . .

While he drove, the wipers swished across the windscreen, spreading the drizzle. The wet weather wasn't making him feel any better, especially with his cold. It had been raining forever, it seemed. The storms had started just after Christmas, and the water came down unrelentingly throughout the month of January and much of February. It was, some said, the most rain the Bay Area had had in years—and desperately needed after a long drought. Even so, with the reservoirs now filled to overflowing and some small towns inundated with flood waters, there were limits to too much of a good thing. It was all a matter of degree. That's what everyone always said, that moderation in everything was the key. That's what Roberta had always argued, even if she didn't always practice what she preached.

In Walnut Creek Jack merged onto Interstate 680 and headed north. In just a few minutes he passed Concord and was on his way into Martinez, where the gray waters of Suisun Bay soon came into view. As he crossed the Benicia Bridge across the east end of the Carquinez Strait, he could see the scores of empty gray ships tied up, bulkhead to bulkhead, masts and superstructures looking like some exotic, unreachable, technical city of the future, even though you knew they were just riding high and empty, useless, mothballed in the backwater. Then farther in the distance, just over the far hill, came the tops of the towers, tanks, and pipe lattices of the refineries behind Benicia, still more outsized technological artforms.

At the north end of the bridge Jack slowed down and passed through the toll booth, handing over the toll coupon and getting a receipt that was time-stamped in return. As soon as he was through the tollgate, Jack swung west onto Interstate 780, and the last mile. At the West Seventh offramp Jack exited once again, and drove under the freeway into the Southampton residential development. From there it was a short distance to home—actually, Roberta's home, a modest green, woodsided condominium that overlooked the freeway.

Jack turned into the asphalt driveway off Sunset Circle

and into the parking space in front of 103 Sunset Circle, Number 7. The time was just after 2 P.M.

Jack crossed the small footbridge that led to the front door. He took out his key and opened it, coming into the living room.

"Mom?" he called out. "I'm home."

Mom didn't answer.

Jack went to his mother's bedroom. The door was slightly open. He pushed it open all the way.

Roberta Butler was lying diagonally across her waterbed, faceup, with the top of her head toward the foot of the bed, rather than toward the headboard. She wasn't moving. A side railing from the bed was on the floor beside the bed. Several stacks of papers were piled on the bed, near Roberta's head.

Jack crossed over to the bedside and put his hand out to touch his mother's face. It was cold. There was no breathing, and Jack knew that she was dead.

At 2:17 that afternoon, Jack called 911. The Benicia Fire Department dispatched its emergency medical team, which arrived just four minutes later. The EMTs found Jack's mother clad only in a pink bathrobe. Like Jack, they detected no pulse or breathing. Rigor mortis had already begun, and lividity—the process of blood draining to the lowest part of the body after death—was well underway. Not only was Roberta Butler definitely dead, she had been dead for some time.

A Benicia police officer who also came to the scene, Tom Dalby, drew Jack into the living room. Dalby looked at Jack.

Dalby saw a good-looking, dark-haired, bearded man, a few inches over six feet, weighing close to 220 pounds. Jack's hands were large, his eyes clear behind his heavily framed glasses. He neither smiled nor frowned. He waited patiently, looking back at Dalby calmly.

What's your name? Dalby asked.

Jack Barron, said Jack.

She's your mother? Dalby asked.

Yes, Jack said.

What's her name?

Roberta, Jack said. Roberta Butler.

She was like this when you found her? Dalby asked.

Yes, just like that, Jack said. I saw her, I said, Mom, but when I touched her, she was cold, so I knew. That's when I called 911.

What time was this, when you found her? Dalby asked.

Just after I got home. Just after two, Jack said.

Was the door locked?

Yes, it was.

Do you live here?

Yes. Since last fall.

When you came in, did you notice anything unusual?

No.

The doors were locked?

Yes.

Dalby now telephoned the Solano County Coroner's Office and requested that a coroner's deputy be put on the line. Coroner's Deputy Stanley Loveless came on. Dalby briefly described the scene. Loveless asked Dalby whether the dead woman had any history of recent illness. Dalby said he didn't know of any. Were there obvious signs of foul play? No, said Dalby.

Let me talk to the son, Loveless said.

Dalby put Jack on the line.

Was your mother under a physician's care?

No, said Jack.

Well, was she taking any medicine?

No.

When was the last time you spoke to your mother?

About ten last night, Jack said. Over the telephone.

Did she have any complaints, anything wrong with her when you talked to her?

She said she was tired, Jack told Loveless. That she felt

weak, and she said she had a headache. She's been under a lot of stress lately.

What kind of stress? Loveless asked.

Job stress, Jack said.

What do you mean?

Well, Jack said, she was a safety director for Safeway Stores. She had to travel a lot, and this was causing her stress.

Anything else?

Yes, Jack said. There were problems in the union, the retail clerks' union, in Vallejo, and that was causing her stress too.

Anything else?

Well, she was depressed.

Loveless considered what he'd learned, then made a decision. In the absence of obvious signs of homicide, he ordered Roberta Butler's body transported to the Coroner's office for a full autopsy and toxicology screen. That would be the first step in trying to find out what happened to Roberta Butler. It was routine in cases when ordinarily healthy people suddenly turned up dead.

But something besides Roberta Butler's recent health history troubled Loveless. His conversation with Jack Barron seemed odd, in some peculiar way—or at least, that's what Loveless thought.

Over the telephone, anyway, Jack seemed flat, unemotional, Loveless believed.

"This writer," Loveless wrote later in his report, "felt that the manner and tone of the deceased's son at that time were unusual for someone who just found out his mother was expired. Mr. Barron appeared to me as though this were an everyday occurrence."

While Jack had been speaking to Loveless, Dalby was hearing something weird from one of the paramedics. Chatting with one of the neighbors, the paramedic had learned some startling information about Jack Barron and Roberta Butler.

Next door to Number 7 one of the paramedics had encountered neighbor Margaret Hawes. Hawes had been shocked to learn that her good friend Roberta Butler was dead.

Oh, this is tragic, just tragic, Hawes told the paramedic. That poor man.

Which poor man? the paramedic asked. Who do you mean?

Why, her son, Hawes said. First his wife, then his son, then his daughter, and now his mother. It's so sad.

Her mind whirling from this casually imparted information, the paramedic pulled Dalby aside and told him what Hawes had said. Dalby now visited Hawes to find out what she meant.

Wait a minute, Dalby said. What's this about his wife, his children? What do you mean?

Dead, too, Hawes told Dalby. All of them dead, one after another. It's just tragic.

Two

Dalby's own brain was well into overdrive when he went back inside the condominium. Jack Barron's wife was dead. His two children were dead. And now *his mother* was dead? Whoa, Dalby said to himself. What's going on here?

Dalby confronted Jack. Jack watched him, still calm.

What's all this about your wife and your children? Dalby asked Jack. Is it true they died? How?

Yes, Jack told Dalby, it was true. First his wife had died, then later his son. No one knew what caused either of the deaths.

They thought it might be something hereditary, or possibly some sort of environmental poisoning, like toxic waste, Jack told Dalby. But, he said, they could never figure out exactly what it was.

The experts were still working on it last summer, Jack added, when my four-year-old, my daughter, Ashley, died too. Nobody's ever been able to say why any of it ever happened.

Jack looked at Dalby.

Where was this? Dalby asked.

Sacramento, Jack said. I come from Sacramento.

SACRAMENTO, CALIFORNIA

Monday, June 8, 1992

Three

The city of Sacramento is California's capital, a 96-square-mile sprawl housing nearly 400,000 souls athwart the American River, where that smaller stream joins the larger, gray-brown Sacramento, one of the largest rivers in the state.

There, in 1839, a Swiss immigrant named Johann Augustes Sutter received a Mexican land grant of 49,000 acres and began laying out a settlement he called New Helvetia.

It was nine years later when a man named James Marshall, one of Sutter's most recent partners, began building a sawmill on the American River some 30 miles upstream from New Helvetia. Prowling the uncompleted millrace one day, Marshall bent down and pried up a small number of yellow fragments from the sediment. With that simple act, the greatest gold rush in history was underway.

Within a year, New Helvetia had become Sacramento, the closest deepwater port to the goldfields of the Sierra Nevada. Every day throughout 1849 and on into the 1850s, hundreds of new immigrants poured upriver from San Francisco and from all other points of the compass, exploding the town's population.

By 1860 the city had become the state capital, and work was started on a large Capitol dome, surrounded by stately

Victorian mansions, all set back from a bustling business district that had grown up along the riverfront.

The city expanded enthusiastically over the next hundred years, adding streets by letter east and west and by number north and south, in an ever-widening grid-like pattern toward the southeast, steadily encroaching on fertile farmland in the flatland to the south and east. Throughout the 1890s, on into the twentieth century, as the Golden State grew ever more prosperous, Sacramento doubled and redoubled in population.

By the end of World War II, as the state government and its bureaucracy exploded in the aftermath of the war, new office buildings began popping up in the downtown core, interspersed with pocket parks, box-like apartment buildings, Chinese laundries, and a heavy sprinkling of bars, restaurants, and saloons, some of the latter notorious for their politician clientele.

By the early 1990s, Sacramento was one of the fastest growing cities in the nation, with a growth rate surpassing 30 percent every ten years. Counting the surrounding area of the entire county, by 1990 the total metropolitan population of the Sacramento metropolitan area was well over 1.1 million residents.

As the city grew in the 1980s, it outstripped its boundaries once more, spilling over into the flat, rich farmland to the south. New residential developments sprouted, leapfrogging their way down the asphalt ribbon of the old military road linking Sacramento to the city of Stockton, some 40 miles away.

It was in one such development, a modest accretion of single-storied, composition-roofed drywalled ramblers, in an unincorporated area of the county called Florin, that a young U.S. Air Force wife and mother, Christina Hamilton, arose early on a muggy morning in June of 1992.

After getting her child up and herself ready to go to work, Christina took her child over to her next-door neighbor's house on Southbreeze Drive. The woman in the neighboring house, Irene, ran a small day-care business, supervising neighborhood children for employed parents like Christina.

Christina knew a little about Irene; after all, it's difficult to live next door to someone without knowing something about them. And, of course, Irene had been taking care of Christina's child for some time, so it was natural for both women to exchange some confidences.

Christina knew that Irene had two children of her own, a son, Jeremy, a bit over three years old, and Ashley, a daughter, a little over two. Christina knew that Irene's husband, Jack, worked late nights and early mornings as a shelf-stocker in a supermarket in east Sacramento. Because of the difference in their schedules, Christina did not see as much of Jack Barron as she did of Irene. As far as she could tell, however, Jack seemed much like everyone else on the block—fairly young, with a working-class job, and with hopes and ambitions common to most growing families trying to stretch a limited paycheck as far as possible.

At 7:10 in the morning Christina knocked on the Barron front door. Receiving no response, Christina knocked again. Again no one answered.

Muttering, Christina returned to her own house with her child. She dialed the Barron telephone number. The phone rang and rang, but went unanswered. Christina guessed something must have happened to interfere with Irene's child-care duties, but thought it a bit strange that Irene hadn't bothered to notify her. In any event, Christina had to get to work.

Leaving her child with friends staying at her house, Christina drove to work. On arriving there, she again called Irene, thinking that perhaps Irene had been distracted earlier, or out. Again the telephone rang, with still no response.

By this point, Christina was worried as well as mystified. What if there was something wrong? Christina decided she had to go back to Irene's house to see if anything was amiss.

Pulling up to the house on Southbreeze Drive shortly after 8 A.M., Christina again knocked on the front door. Again receiving no response, Christina tried to open the door but found it locked. Moving around the side of the house, Christina tried the side doors, then the windows, each time trying to find a way to get inside. As she moved around the house, she realized that she could hear someone inside.

It was Jeremy, Christina realized. Tapping on one of the windows, Christina got Jeremy's attention. After a few minutes she coaxed Jeremy into opening a sliding glass door at the rear of the house. To open the door, Jeremy removed a small dowel from the sliding track, which ordinarily blocked its passage.

Jeremy looked up at Christina.

"I can't wake my mommy up," he told her.

Christina went through the house until she came to the rear bedroom, the one shared by Irene and Jack. As she came into the room, trailed by both Jeremy and Ashley, Christina realized almost at once that something was very wrong.

Irene lay back on the Barrons' waterbed, feet on the floor. She was wearing a pink nightgown and pink panties. Her feet were encased in fuzzy pink slippers. The strangest thing was Irene's face. It was covered with a bed pillow.

"Irene?" Christina called out. Irene didn't move. Christina went to the bed and removed the pillow from Irene's face. Irene's left arm extended across her chest to the right, with the back of the left hand lying palm-up on the bed; her right arm lay extended by her side. Her face was turned toward the right. Christina saw blood on a pillow underneath Irene's head, and more blood that had trickled down from Irene's nose. Irene's eyes were fixed and the pupils were dilated. To Christina, Irene appeared to be dead.

Quickly backing out of the bedroom, Christina told Jeremy and Ashley to go to their bedrooms. Trying to quell her panic, Christina dialed 911.

Christina told the operator about Irene. The operator asked Christina if she could perform cardiopulmonary resuscitation, or CPR. Christina put the phone down and went back into the bedroom. She tried moving Irene's arms, but the arms were rigid.

Christina went back to the telephone and reported the situation to the operator. Please stay there, Christina was told; the paramedics are on the way.

In a major metropolitan area like Sacramento, thousands of people die every year. Some die in car wrecks; some commit suicide; many die in hospitals, prey to myriad natural causes that limit even the longest life span. And some, of course, are murdered.

With so many deaths, it's not surprising that government authorities have devised a process for dealing with unexpected death. The shock troops of the process—those who respond first—are the paramedics, the emergency medical technicians, frequently employed by local fire departments. On that morning in June of 1992, the first to arrive on Southbreeze Drive were paramedics from the Florin Fire District.

The firemen were admitted to the house by Christina, who showed them Irene's body in the back bedroom. Then Christina took Jeremy and Ashley over to her house, and then returned to the Barron house to wait for the police to arrive.

The emergency medical personnel quickly concluded that there was nothing they could do for Irene; as Christina had realized, Irene was beyond any medical help. Now the ball was in the hands of the patrol officers from the Sacramento County Sheriff's Department, who had arrived shortly after the Florin EMTs.

The two patrol officers, Mark Freeman and Mitchell Boyes, looked over the bedroom and Irene's body. They noted her dress, and most of all, the pillow that Christina had said she'd removed from Irene's face. While there was no overt evidence of foul play—no gunshot wound, no substantial blood, no apparent bruising, no visible evidence of strangulation—the death of an otherwise apparently healthy 34-year-old woman was nonetheless an unusual event. The patrol officers decided to activate the next level of death response—they called the Sheriff's Department's homicide detectives, just to be sure.

Sheriff's detectives Rick Lauther and Bob Riesdorph soon arrived, to be briefed by the patrol officers, the EMTs, and Christina. The detectives walked through the house and found nothing to indicate that anyone had broken in. Questioning Christina, they learned that all the doors had been locked, and that she had only gotten inside after Jeremy removed the dowel from the sliding door track.

By this point, Southbreeze Drive was crowded with emergency vehicles—the EMT van, the Sheriff's patrol cars, the detectives' car, and an ambulance.

Thus it was, at about 9:30 A.M., that Jack Barron drove down his street toward his house, only to see a hum of ominous activity in front.

Jack parked his car on the opposite side of the street and began walking toward the front door. Christina must have identified Jack for the detectives as he approached, because Detective Lauther met Jack halfway across the street.

Mr. Barron? Lauther asked.

Yes, Jack said. I'm Jack Barron.

Lauther told Jack that his wife, Irene, had been found dead that morning by their neighbor, Christina Hamilton. Jack seemed staggered by this news, so much so that Lauther had to keep him from collapsing in the street. Jack said he didn't understand. He began to cry. He wanted to go into the house, but Lauther prevented him. Jack asked Lauther how Irene had died. Lauther said, it wasn't clear yet, but that it appeared to be from natural causes.

Jack asked about Jeremy and Ashley, but Lauther assured him they were being taken care of by Christina. Then Lauther asked Jack some questions.

You were at work last night?

Yes, Jack said.

Where do you work?

Lucky's Supermarket.

You worked all night? ·

Yes.

What time did you leave to go to work?

Around eleven.

Did you see Irene at any time after that?

No, I was at work.

She was all right when you last saw her?

Yes.

Any medical problems?

Not that I know of, Jack said. She'd had a little cold recently, and had been coughing a bit. A few headaches but nothing really bad.

To Lauther, it seemed that Jack was suffering real grief and shock at the death of his wife. He asked Jack to go over to Christina's house and wait for him; there was more the police had to do in the house.

The question was: how did Irene die? When Lauther added it all up, nothing was very clear. There were no obvious signs of trauma on the body—no gunshot wounds, no stab wounds, no stocking knotted around the neck—and it seemed clear the house had been securely locked against all intruders. Still, the whole situation seemed a bit suspicious. Perhaps an expert opinion might clarify matters.

At that point, Lauther and Reisdorph activated the next level in the death response protocol, as they understood it: they called the Sacramento County Coroner's Office and asked for the on-duty forensic pathologist. Dr. Gregory Schmunk took this call from Reisdorph. Reisdorph told him that they had a "possible scene," Schmunk reported later. The fact that Reisdorph asked for a forensic pathologist to come to the scene was unusual; generally, in a county that performed as many as 1,000 autopsies a year, forensic pathologists waited in the laboratory for the dead to be brought to them, and Reisdorph certainly knew this.

But in requesting the presence of a pathologist, Reisdorph appears to have been asking for professional help in deciding just how the detectives should next proceed. At the time, however, Schmunk told Reisdorph to call the Coroner's Office directly and talk to a coroner's investigator and let the investigator decide whether Schmunk's services were needed.

Coroner's investigator Bob Brian then received this call from Reisdorph, just as Lauther finished talking with Jack. Brian consulted with Schmunk, and after some discussion, the two decided to go to the Southbreeze house as Reisdorph had requested. They arrived about 10 A.M.

At the house, Schmunk and Brian entered the bedroom, and found Irene, as described, lying on her back on the bed, feet on the floor. Three pillows were on the bed around her head, including the one with the apparent blood stains found under Irene's head by Christina Hamilton.

The detectives briefed Schmunk. They said they had learned from Jack and Christina Hamilton that Irene had been suffering a series of headaches over the weekend. Christina recalled that while shopping with Irene on Saturday, Irene had slurred her speech.

Schmunk's examination of Irene began at 10:15 A.M. He noted the almost complete rigidity of the extremities and the jaw; moreover, he noted that the lividity—the downward draining of the body's blood after death—was fixed, meaning that the draining process had been completed hours earlier. The body was cold to the touch, with the exception of a slightly warmer area in the midsection. Schmunk and Brian put plastic bags around Irene's hands to preserve any possible evidence that might have been caught up under her fingernails.

Schmunk now turned his attention to the pillows. One pillow—the one with blood—was on the bed above Irene's head. A second was lying next to the right hand, and a third along the left side of the body. This last pillow, Schmunk thought, appeared to have been the one Christina said she had found over Irene's face. The pillow had black streaks on it, which Schmunk thought might be from eye makeup. He noted that Irene did appear to be wearing dark eye makeup.

Schmunk looked closer at Irene's face. He noticed a number of tiny broken blood vessels in Irene's eyes. He saw no other injuries besides what appeared to be a bruise on the back of the right calf.

Schmunk took the ambient temperature of the bed surface around Irene, and recorded it as 79 degrees. A few minutes later he cut an incision in Irene's side and took a liver temperature of 91 degrees.

As a general rule, a dead body loses its heat at a rate of approximately one-half a degree per hour, less if the environment is quite warm. Assuming that Irene had had a normal temperature of 98.6 at the time she died, that was an indication that Irene had died as long as 15 hours earlier. The extent of the rigor mortis and the fixed lividity seemed to support that indication as well.

Counting backward from 10:30 A.M. would therefore put the time of Irene's death at as early as 7:30 P.M. the night before, perhaps slightly later because of the temperature of the waterbed. But that wasn't possible: hadn't Jack said he'd seen Irene alive and well at about 11 P.M. as he left for work?

The truth is, despite the time-honored tradition of English country house murder mysteries, in which the culprit is invariably unmasked by the clever exposure of a bogus alibi for the exact time of the murder, in the real world fixing the time of death is a notoriously difficult undertaking. Most medical examiners, in fact, don't even attempt to do it; they frequently consider the time of death to be somewhere between the time a person is last seen and the time the body is discovered.

But with a cold, rigid body in a locked house, found with

bedroom slippers on, and *still wearing eye makeup*, there could be only one conclusion—that Irene Barron died before going to bed the night before. The question was: exactly when?

Did she die after Jack left for work, or before?

And what about the pillow? How had it gotten over her face?

Schmunk did not consider the pillow that Christina had removed from Irene's body directly indicative of foul play; sometimes, he told the detectives, people suffering from headaches pull pillows over their faces to shut out the light and ease the pain.

Still, these results of Schmunk's on-scene examination should have fired the suspicions of everyone present at the Southbreeze house that day, particularly the suggestive evidence about the possible time of death. That they did not was to set the stage for untold pain and confusion for three entire families for three long years.

Four

While Schmunk had doubts about Irene's death, he wasn't paid for that; rather, he was a scientist, whose job it was to discover the facts, not guesses, of exactly how Irene had died.

If Schmunk could show that the death was a natural result of illness, for example, there would be no point to voicing any suspicions, and Jack would be spared the added trauma of being investigated for possible murder. Schmunk told the detectives to hold off until he completed a thorough autopsy, and the two detectives readily agreed to wait; after all, they had plenty of other cases to work in which the cause of death was quite obvious.

Irene's body was removed to the Sacramento County Coroner's Office, then located in seriously overcrowded quarters near the University of California, Davis, Medical Center, at 44 R Street in south Sacramento.

When Irene's body arrived at the coroner's, attendants wheeled it through the doors into a large cold room—the "cooler," as the coroner's staff referred to it. There, racked on metal tiers stretching from floor to ceiling, were scores of dead bodies, each awaiting some form of final, official disposition. Each was concealed in the same identical plastic shroud, their only remaining individual characteristic the single big toe protruding from the gray plastic bag, to which had been attached the appropriate tag.

The sheer number of corpses in such a place is disquieting, when one realizes one is outnumbered by the dead. It isn't possible to enter a big city morgue without becoming acutely aware of the fragile, and all-too-often unanticipated, boundary between living and dying; eventually one is forced to recall that this unfathomably mysterious destination, death, is everyone's ultimate fate—right down to the impersonality of the toe tag.

Schmunk began the autopsy of toe tag number 92-1930, Irene Barron, that same afternoon. He was assisted by a staff of three. Detectives Lauther and Reisdorph were witnesses.

The mere recording of an autopsy report, larded as it is with arcane medical terminology and Latinate phrases, does not begin to give an idea of the incredible violence done to a human body during an autopsy. In short, the body is literally taken apart with knives, saws, and pry bars. Skin is peeled back, layer by layer, until raw bone is exposed; internal organs such as the heart, the lungs, the stomach, the kidneys, the liver, the brain, are all removed and often dissected and sometimes even pureed in a blender to obtain samples needed for testing.

In short, a forensic pathologist is something like a master mechanic. By taking the body apart, by stripping it down to its component parts, the pathologist strives to discern just how life left.

Schmunk began his autopsy by more closely inspecting the body, which had just been washed. As he inspected, Schmunk took a number of print photographs with a 35-millimeter camera equipped with a closeup lens. In the better light of the pathology laboratory, Schmunk now noticed some things he hadn't seen at the house.

For one thing, Schmunk noticed a band of red spots running from the right side of the mouth to the back of the neck. The pattern of spots was approximately an inch wide and about six inches long. These were "Tardieu" spots—blood hemorrhages under the skin. What caused the spots? It was impossible for Schmunk to say with certainty, although he thought it was possible that the hemorrhages had occurred after death as the blood settled on the right side of Irene's face.

A closer look at the face showed quite a number of similar, smaller spots, particularly on the right side of the face. There were additional small hemorrhages inside the mouth, and a larger area of bleeding inside the right lower lip.

Schmunk inspected the fingernails and found no foreign material, which might have been expected if Irene had scratched an assailant.

Schmunk now noticed a number of bruises on Irene's body that he hadn't noted at the Southbreeze house. One was a blue, green, and red bruise on the upper right arm. Another bruise, which Schmunk thought might be somewhat older, was in the right armpit. Schmunk took sections of each area for testing and microscopic inspection.

Similarly, Schmunk now noticed bruising on the backs of Irene's right index and middle fingers, and a scraping of the back of the left thumb and index finger. A Band-Aid covered a cut on the left middle finger.

Schmunk now measured the bruise on the back of the right calf, which was about two inches by six inches. He also noticed bruising on the bottom and side of the right foot. Schmunk took tissue sections of these areas as well.

Finally, Schmunk noticed several slight, curved reddish indentations behind the ears.

At that point, Schmunk began his internal examination. When it was over, Schmunk had found several areas of hemorrhage inside the neck and throat, as well as over a portion of the interior surface of the lungs.

Schmunk removed Irene's brain for later examination by a neuropathologist.

The rest of Irene's internal organs, however—the heart,

the liver, the kidneys—everything seemed utterly normal. After everything was done, Schmunk took the film out of the camera and put it in an envelope for filing.

At this point, the detectives wanted to know what killed Irene.

I don't know, Schmunk said.

Five

If Detectives Lauther and Reisdorph were disappointed at Schmunk's answer, they were not surprised. As veteran detectives, they knew that it wasn't always possible for pathologists to determine a cause of death with precision.

But Schmunk wasn't ready to give up so quickly. He noted that further microscopic examination of various tissues taken in the autopsy might provide an answer, as could a variety of toxicology tests.

If, for example, analysis of Irene's blood and tissues showed traces of a drug or rare disease or poison, that might clarify matters. And there was still the examination of the brain to go; something might turn up there to explain why a seemingly healthy 34-year-old mother of two would simply drop dead for no apparent reason.

Reisdorph and Lauther asked about the hemorrhaging and the bruises. Wasn't that evidence of something, like maybe violence? Both detectives knew, from previous experience, that the small petechial hemorrhages found in Irene's eyes and on her face and in her lungs were indications of possible asphyxiation. Such bursting blood vessels often occur as blood pressure increases while the body is being starved for oxygen.

But not always, Schmunk said. You can't be sure that the hemorrhaging didn't take place because of a death by natural causes. You can often find the same sort of petechia in deaths other than by violent causes; it might well be part of the agonal dying process, the result of a heart attack or brain seizure or some other cause. These hemorrhages are normal findings, he said; non-specific to any one kind of death.

And as for the bruises, he added, who knows when they occurred? They might have no connection with the death at all.

But could it still be murder? Reisdorph and Lauther asked, persisting.

Sure, said Schmunk. But right now, don't expect me to say it is. Until we get more information, I'm not saying anything anywhere near close to something like *that*. I'll let you know what the other tests come up with, if anything.

With this, Lauther and Reisdorph went back to their office on G Street in downtown Sacramento to fill out their reports. With the absence of a cause of death, there was no point to investigating any further. Until a forensic pathologist was willing to swear in court that Irene Barron had died as a result of an act of homicidal violence, there was no case to investigate. That was the policy of the Sacramento Sheriff's Department, which had, Lord knew, enough to do without begging for more.

Six

Later—much later—this policy of the Sacramento Sheriff's Department was to be the subject of fierce contention between the Sheriff's Department and the Sacramento Coroner's Office.

The Sheriff's Department insisted that it was fruitless for them to pursue a criminal investigation in the absence of a cause of death; while the Coroner's Office eventually insisted, in the light of subsequent events, that an investigation by the Sheriff's Department might actually help *establish* the cause of death.

This chicken-and-egg conundrum was to bedevil both agencies for the better part of three years, while the death of Irene Barron slumbered in the cracks of the Sacramento County criminal justice system.

In retrospect, it appears that the Coroner's Office had the better part of the argument. For, had the Sheriff's Department initiated a serious investigation of the circumstances of Irene Barron's death that spring, the chances are quite good that three other people might be alive today.

For one thing, insulated by the medical mystification of Schmunk, neither Lauther nor Reisdorph bothered to find out very much about Jack Barron, or the circumstances of the Barron family life before Irene Barron died. Had they inquired, they might well have discovered a number of facts that would have given them pause before deciding that Irene Barron's death was none of their affair.

Nor did anyone consider some of the hidden, yet most astounding, coincidences in the lives of Irene Barron, Jack Barron, and their families—synchronicities that, if not necessarily directly indicative of what really happened to Irene that June night and morning, were at the very least powerful evidence of some sort of mysterious force that somehow pulls people together, in some sort of hardly understood yet still fated way—for good or ill.

Because, when it came to the lives of Irene and Jack Barron, there were by far too many otherwise meaningless coincidences: of names, of dates, of places, almost as if some controlling force had mixed up two families' lives in some sort of macabre cosmic joke.

JACK AND IRENE

1961–1992

Seven

Jack Kenneth Barron was born October 21, 1961, in Castro Valley, California, the only son of Elmore J. Barron, then 22, and his wife, the 19-year-old former Roberta Ann Leoni.

Young Elmore married Roberta on December 30 of the year before, 1960, in Reno, Nevada. Roberta was just 18 at the time of the marriage.

Whether the experience of Roberta's becoming pregnant so soon after their marriage unnerved the two young parents, or for whatever other reason, there were no Barron siblings to follow. Later, both Jack and Roberta were to contend that Elmore always maintained he was sterile, and so could not have been Jack's real father. Roberta angrily denied that she had slept with any other man, either before or after marrying Elmore.

Roberta was a staunch Catholic girl, the daughter of Eugene Leoni and his wife, Edith, longtime residents of the North Bay area. By the accounts of those who knew her, Roberta seems to have been a very strong-willed person with definite, even rigid ideas of what was appropriate behavior. She also, as she grew older, came to believe deeply in signs, omens, and portents, and became devoted to astrology; indeed, some who knew her did not hesitate in describing Roberta as superstitious.

As the early sixties unfolded, Elmore, Roberta, and little Jack moved to Orange County in Southern California, where Elmore obtained work on the Southern Pacific Railroad. There Jack attended elementary school and the first years of junior high school, all of those grades in the strictest Roman Catholic tradition.

Despite this religious presence, by the early 1970s the marriage between Elmore and Roberta was in terminal trouble. Roberta objected to Elmore's frequent absences, while Elmore grew more withdrawn from his wife. Jack watched these power struggles almost as if he were an unseen spectator as far as Elmore and Roberta were concerned, at least according to those who knew Elmore and Roberta.

Judging from those observations, and from those who came to know him, it appears that Jack was heavily influenced, albeit in quite different ways, by both his father and his mother. He admired Elmore, and perhaps even envied him, right down to wanting to emulate his career as a railroad man. At the same time it also appears that Elmore was a distant figure in his son's life, a stern, even forbidding presence.

In an anecdote that was as revealing of Elmore as it was of Jack, Elmore was to recall that Jack was "fastidious" as much about his behavior as his person or surroundings.

"Maybe Jack got part of that from me, because I used to come home from work and see him leaning against my car with his foot on the bumper or something," Elmore was to tell the *Sacramento Bee* newspaper years later.

"I have a rough voice anyway, and I would tell him, 'Get your foot off that bumper, it wasn't put there for you to prop up on.' And I had expensive cars, like Mercedes and Volvos."

Other than setting such arbitrary and seemingly petty rules, one does not get the sense that Elmore was much involved emotionally in his son's life, except to demonstrate his power as a locomotive engineer. There are no anecdotes about father-son activities, like a trip to a ball game or camping out overnight; no Boy Scouts, no mutual hobbies or interests, no real interest in "Jackie," as Elmore persisted in calling his son even into Jack's thirties, as anything other than an appendage of Elmore.

Certainly, there is no evidence that Elmore did much to groom his son as to what it meant to be a man.

Instead, it appears that much of Jack's upbringing was left to Roberta. By all accounts, Roberta doted on Jack— just as long as Jack conformed to what Roberta believed were appropriate standards of behavior, which were sharply defined by Roberta's religion.

"She waited on him hand and foot," an acquaintance was to recall later, even into Jack's adulthood. And when Jack occasionally rebelled against Roberta's standards, Roberta was quick to offer blandishments designed to bring Jack back under her control-by-servitude.

As a staunch Catholic, Roberta had very strong ideas of morality, and she endeavored mightily to see that Jack embodied those ideals. For Roberta and hence Jack, church attendance was a very prominent, even mandatory activity. And at the same time, Jack's personality seemed to subsume something of Roberta's; even years later, some of Jack's acquaintances would remark on the slight undertone of femininity in Jack's personality. For all his size, it seemed to some that Jack was the quintessential "mama's boy."

As a result of these influences, there grew in Jack a number of contradictory impulses: on one hand, admiration of his father, both for Elmore's dominating personality and for the way Elmore stood up to the ubiquitously powerful Roberta, coupled to an unrequited boyhood yearning for respect from Elmore; on the other, dependence on and resentment of his mother, who provided his emotional needs and the behavioral model he needed to adhere to in order to maintain this emotional support.

All of these contradictory impulses were brought to the surface when, in the mid-seventies, the marriage of Elmore and Roberta finally shattered. As Elmore was to describe it later, this time it was Roberta who accused Elmore of sexual infidelity. Elmore became angry at Roberta and denied this.

When Roberta persisted in her accusations, Elmore told her that since he couldn't convince her otherwise, he might as well leave that very night. And so he did, walking away from the marriage and "Jackie" without a single backward glance.

Later Elmore was to estimate that he had seen Jack no more than three times over the next two decades.

Furious and bitter, Roberta left Orange County and returned to her roots in the Bay Area, taking then 13-year-old Jack with her. Both mother and son were impoverished, a condition Roberta frequently and vociferously blamed on the "irresponsibility" of Elmore, who, in Roberta's view, was more interested in playing around with other women than in taking responsibility for his son. From that point forward, Jack was given to understand by his mother that his father was a worthless, irresponsible, duplicitous cretin who didn't give a damn about Jack.

Losing one's male parental role model, even one as remote as Elmore appears to have been, would be difficult enough for any 13-year-old. For Jack, the loss was made even more difficult by the move north, which thrust him into strange surroundings, into new schools, where he knew no one and no one knew him. The separation also increased Roberta's influence over Jack. Survivors of the Elmore wreckage, they became even more dependent on one another.

Roberta went on welfare for a time, and had to sue Elmore for $2,000 in back financial support. Finally, in the late 1970s, things began to stabilize when Roberta got a job as a Safeway produce clerk. One thing led to another, and Roberta fell in love with the store's assistant manager,

Bob Butler. By the end of the 1970s, Roberta and Butler were married. By then, also, Jack was ready to graduate from high school, and to face the daunting prospect of living on his own.

Eight

If Jack's family life met the classic definition of dysfunctional, quite the opposite could be said of Irene.

Born as the fourth and last child of Jack and Norma Paget, Irene grew up in a family that was supportive, loving, and extremely close-knit. With an older sister and two older brothers, Irene was always seen as the baby of the family, as indulged as she was loved. From all the descriptions of Irene that friends and relatives were later to give of her, the overwhelming impression is of someone who never really had any grasp of how duplicitous people can sometimes be; it was, it seems, Irene's basic nature to trust people.

Irene was born at St. Mary's Hospital in Reno, Nevada, on July 18, 1957, when her father, Jack Paget, was serving in the U.S. Air Force. Jack Paget was a radar specialist, a career Air Force man who had joined the Air Force as a young kid out of Pasadena, California, in the early 1940s. Young Jack became a tailgunner on a B-17 bomber, and some, perhaps even he, thought he had the world by the tail in 1943. But somewhere over Germany in the summer of 1944, Jack Paget's bomber was shot out of the sky, and Jack Paget had to bail out, forced to become a man, ready or not.

Captured by the Germans, Jack was sent to a POW camp, where he spent the remainder of World War II either freezing or starving, or usually both. Years later, he could still recall freezing his feet on a forced march from one Stalag to another in the dead of winter.

But in the end, the camps were liberated, and Jack Paget returned to his country in the summer of 1945. By winter of that year he had met a beautiful young woman from Colorado and had fallen in love. Married in December of 1945 to Norma, by November of 1946, Jack and Norma were the parents of their first-born child, John, born in Norma's home state of Colorado in November of 1946.

After a short stint with the Post Office in Colorado, Jack Paget decided to go back into the Air Force, just then expanding as the Cold War began to freeze in earnest. By 1948 Jack and Norma were parents to another son, Paul, born in 1948, in Washington State.

Soon the Paget family was moving from billet to billet as Jack Paget developed his expertise in the rapidly expanding field of radar signal assessment; the service assignments took the Paget family from Washington State to Oakland, California, where a daughter, Debra, was born during the Korean War; and after that to Reno, where Irene came into the world in 1957.

As was common for many service families, the Pagets moved frequently during the Cold War, traveling from base to base as the need required. In one year alone, John Paget was later to recall, he attended seven different schools, including two in Washington State, two in Colorado, and three in Germany. With such frequent disruptions, it wasn't at all unusual that the children of the Paget family formed deep and close attachments to one another; the family was the one constant in a life of permanent change.

By 1964, the Pagets settled in Riverside, California. Baby Irene was then eight years old, and Father Jack was on the edge of gaining his 20-year Air Force retirement. After separation from the service, Jack spent a few months

as a prison guard, then found another slot with the Post
Office. By the late sixties, the Pagets had moved to Fallbrook, California, an idyllic small town in the foothills halfway between Los Angeles and San Diego. By this time
Irene was a teenager, and about to take her first steps into
adulthood.

Much later, John Paget was to recall his little sister, Irene.
To John, Irene was never the smartest whip, but she had
always been honest and straightforward. From the earliest
time John could remember, Irene always had the sweetest,
most even temper of all the Pagets. It was if she had been
born calm and loving.

John himself hadn't always gotten along that well with
his father, Jack Paget; in fact, John had run away from his
father's Air Force assignment in Riverside in 1965 to be
with his high school sweetheart in Reno. Jack and Norma
were exasperated, but within a few months John and his
high school love were married, and even if Jack Paget
wanted his first-born son's impulsive marriage annulled, it
wasn't going to happen; Norma saw to that.

John spent the next few years in Reno, going to college
and learning accounting, while Irene was growing into
adulthood; by the early 1970s, when Jack Paget began a
part-time income tax business in Fallbrook to supplement
his Post Office pay and his Air Force pension, son John,
by now a CPA, and his own growing family were ready to
relocate. By that time little Irene was in high school, a
beautiful child who was on the way to becoming an even
more beautiful young woman.

Irene wasn't much interested in school, as John recalled
later.

"She spent her high school years here in Fallbrook,"
John said. "There's nothing here to do. I mean, this is not
downtown San Diego. She loved animals. She had lots of
pets—rabbits and dogs and cats. She had a horse my father
got her, that she was scared to death of.

"I remember helping her with her high school book-keeping. She and her friend Denise Eikmeier would come over to the house after school to get my help. Irene had a hard time with it, she just couldn't understand bookkeeping. She was on the banner team, and marched with the high school band. In her senior year, she ran for Miss Fallbrook, at my father's urging. To him, she was daddy's little girl, the most beautiful little girl in all of Fallbrook, so of course she would win. And she did."

Irene's main interest, John thought, was boys. What Irene most wanted was to get married and start raising a family.

"She wanted to be Norma Paget," John said later. "She wanted to be her mother, to have a husband and a home and start taking care of babies."

After graduating from Fallbrook High in 1975, Irene had not the slightest interest in attending college. Instead, she grew close to her high school boyfriend, Keith. Within a year or so of graduation, Irene and Keith married.

Sadly, for Irene, the marriage did not last.

"He left her, she didn't leave him," John recalled. "It came as somewhat of a surprise to her. She didn't realize, she professed (later) that she really didn't understand the degree to which Keith was unhappy in the marriage."

The failure of the marriage in 1985 devastated Irene, according to John.

"Having been raised in a family where you married once for life, and you stick it out through thick and thin, I think Irene was somewhat embarrassed and guilt-ridden that the marriage didn't work," John said later.

After a year or so knocking around Fallbrook and dating a few men, Irene decided she needed a change of scenery. She, along with her best friend, Denise, decided to go to Sacramento in January of 1986.

Years later, John was still unsure why Irene and Denise decided to go to Sacramento rather than, say, San Francisco or Los Angeles. But Denise knew.

"We wanted a bigger town," Denise was to recall. "San

Diego was too expensive, and nobody wants to live in Los Angeles.'' Besides, Irene had a cousin living in Sacramento. Denise and Irene moved north, and both obtained jobs as secretaries, Irene in an insurance office.

As it turned out, choosing Sacramento was a fateful decision: because of that choice she was to meet a large, strapping man, four years younger than she was: the then 24-year-old Jack Kenneth Barron.

Nine

His mother's marriage to Bob Butler in 1979 resulted in more changes in Jack Barron's life. After having lived in Suisun City, near Roberta's mother in Fairfield, the now-expanded family moved across the Carquinez Strait to the small town of Port Costa, where the newly married Butlers managed a jewelry shop part-time. Jack, who had been attending Armijo High School in the Suisun area, now transferred to John Swett High School in Crockett, a few miles away from Port Costa.

The new school seems to have intimidated Jack. Later, his aunt, Jeanne Dillon—Roberta's sister—recalled that Jack was a loner during his last year in high school, without any real friends. Certainly he had no girlfriends, if one didn't count Roberta.

Still, Jack was a better-than-average student, graduating from Swett with a 3.05 grade point average in 1980. After graduation, Jack continued to live with Roberta and Bob and eventually found work in the supermarket industry, as they had.

The supermarket business was all right, but Jack still wanted to be like his own father, Elmore. Eventually, through a mutual friend of Roberta and Elmore who worked for the Union Pacific, Jack was able to get a job with the railroad as a laborer in 1984. That job lasted for almost two years, until Jack suffered a knee injury while at work. He filed a disability claim, got paid, and left the railroad in January 1986.

The following month, while visiting Dave Bednarczyk, a longtime acquaintance of Elmore and Roberta's who lived near Mount Shasta, Jack met Irene for the first time.

Like Elmore, Dave worked for the railroad, which was how he met Elmore and Roberta in the first place. After Elmore and Roberta divorced, it appears that Dave was the closest thing to a male role model Jack had—almost a sort of older brother; in fact, Jack was in later years to refer to Dave as his brother.

In one of those twists of fate, Dave had some years earlier met and married a longtime friend of Irene Paget's, also from Fallbrook: a woman named Patty Marlin. In February of 1986, Irene and Denise Eikmeier went to Shasta to visit Patty, and were introduced to Jack.

"They kept telling us about this guy they wanted Irene to meet," Denise said later, speaking of Jack.

Denise remembered the weekend at Shasta fondly.

"We had a nice weekend," she said. Jack was funny, and impressed Irene as someone who knew how to treat a lady. Denise was surprised, not only at Jack's youth—he was four years younger than Irene—but also that Irene seemed attracted to him.

"He didn't seem to be Irene's type, but they hit it off real fast," Denise said. "On the Saturday we met, I was helping Patty with the dishes, and we needed something, I forget what. Jack and Irene went to the store together, and they were gone for a long time, far longer than necessary. They were sitting in the car talking. Well, they just hit it off. He wasn't like anyone she'd ever dated before. Usually she went for guys who were older, more sophisticated. Jack was young, immature. He wore plaid flannel shirts like he was a lumberjack."

But Jack was eager to please Irene, and after the unhappiness with Keith, Jack's attentions meant much to Irene.

"He put her on a pedestal," Denise recalled. "Her exhusband didn't do that. That's what attracted her to him. She thought, 'He's so young I can mold him.' "

At this time, Jack was still living with Roberta and Bob, now in Vallejo, taking treatment for his knee injury. Soon Jack and Irene were dating, however, with Jack driving in on Fridays from Vallejo, and staying at the apartment shared by Irene and Denise until Sunday night. Over the next few weeks, Jack began spending more and more time at the apartment, arriving on Thursdays, then leaving on Mondays.

"Slowly but surely he was there full-time," Denise remembered. The two women nicknamed Jack "Jacko," which he hated. But they persisted, and the nickname eventually stuck.

Finally, in November of 1986, the three decided to rent a three-bedroom house in Sacramento—one room for Irene and Jack, one for Denise, and a third for Jack's train collection. Irene, Denise and Jack flew down to San Diego, rented a trailer, and loaded up all of Irene and Denise's worldly possessions, including Irene's pet poodle, Suzy, for the trip north.

By any account, Jack was an avid train buff.

"He was a train fanatic," Denise recalled. "We had to get a three-bedroom house, and one room was just for his trains. He had tall filing cabinets, and they were stuffed with some train magazine. He got two copies every month. One was never opened, just filed away. The other he'd use to tear out articles, cut out pictures, mark it up, that sort of thing. He was always buying and selling and trading model railroad cars with other collectors around the country. Some of these were worth hundreds of dollars. He had a stack of boxes, color slides of trains and cars, thousands of them; he had a bookshelf full of train books and memorabilia from trains, like a phone used on a train, or train signs. Anyway, this room had nothing but trains.''

Denise thought Jack's obsessive fascination with railroads was a way of being close to his absent father, Elmore.

Only three months after signing a year lease on the three-bedroom house, in early 1987, Jack and Irene decided to move to Mount Shasta, to be near Jack's friend/brother Dave, and his wife Patty. Denise was furious at being stuck with a house she couldn't afford. She made Jack pay the entire rent until a new tenant could be found, and found her own apartment.

Denise believed that Irene agreed to the move to Shasta because Jack was lonely in Sacramento, and wanted to be near his friend Dave. Denise thought Jack was afflicted with a bad case of hero worship.

"Dave was Jack's best friend," Denise recalled. "Jack was like a little boy, and Dave could tell Jack to jump off a cliff, and Jack would do it. He was starving for attention, and here was this older guy who gave him all this attention. Whatever Dave said, Jack kind of went with it.''

Irene was eventually to regret the move, according to Denise. She and Dave soon entered into a battle for control of Jack's soul.

"Irene didn't like Patty and Dave, but she put up with them because of Jack," Denise said. "She tolerated Dave, tried to be friendly.'' But Irene, according to Denise, thought that Dave had far too much influence over Jack.

After living with Jack at Shasta from early 1987 into the spring of 1988, Irene discovered she was pregnant. That July, she and Jack decided to get married.

For the Paget family, the news of Irene's decision to re-marry was quite welcome. The whole family had felt badly for Irene when her first marriage failed, and was hopeful that this new marriage would provide her with the home and stability she longed for.

The Pagets—Jack and Norma, John and his wife, and

John's children—drove the Paget family motor home north from Fallbrook for the wedding, where they would meet Jack Barron for the first time.

"You know," John said later, "you always have first impressions. And we stepped out of the motor home, my wife and me and my two kids, and my parents. We pull up in a motor home and we step out. And we're greeted by Irene and this big, clumsy-looking character. And it comes in contrast with who she'd been married to before. Keith was much more slight in his build than Jack, and certainly more handsome. My first reaction to Jack was, this is just a dumb kid. What does she see in him?"

John's first reaction to Jack was a sinking feeling that Irene had found herself tied up with someone so unsuitable. But John must have hidden his feelings well, because Jack took to the Pagets as if he'd known them all his life.

"But he was very outgoing," John said. "And he was marrying Irene, so we're instantly all family. And it's hugs and kisses. He was quite gregarious, and I [said to myself] well, you know, I'll probably learn to like this guy, he's okay. Certainly Irene seems to be happy and that's what counts. I never thought much more about it after that."

What was more surprising, though, was that John was pressed into serving as Jack's best man in the wedding ceremony. Dave had been scheduled for the job, but at the last minute the Bednarcyzks pulled out of the ceremony.

"Patty was pissed off because Irene wasn't going to have Patty as the maid of honor," John recalled. "Patty thought she'd be the maid of honor because she had introduced them. But Irene's going to have her best friend be maid of honor, and that's Denise. As I understand the story, Irene wanted Patty to be a bridesmaid, but that wasn't good enough. They got in a huff. Next thing you know, Dave's calling Jack, you know, I can't be in the wedding. When I show up, I get a phone call: Can you be Jack's best man?"

So John performed as the best man of the groom at the wedding of his little sister Irene.

Also present at the wedding, of course, was Roberta, who by then had ended her own marriage to Bob Butler. To John, Roberta seemed the completely doting mother, intensely interested in her son and his welfare. At one point, in fact, before the wedding, Roberta showed up at the house Irene and Jack were sharing while both Irene and Jack were out, and proceeded to rearrange all the living room furniture.

Irene was appalled, according to her brother.

"She told Jack something to the effect, I can't have this, I mean this is not going to work. Your mother is not going to come over and rearrange furniture when we're gone. So I guess at Irene's insistence, Jack had a talk with [Roberta]. Now my recollection is, I think it happened a second time. I'm not sure whether she insisted Jack step in after the second time it happened or after the first time, but I know that at some point Irene put her foot down and said, 'This isn't going to happen.'. And Irene was not the kind to be that assertive, normally, so it must have really tweaked her."

Still, it was John's impression of his sister that she never would have confronted Roberta directly about her unthinking interference.

"I think Irene's approach would have been to Jack, something like, 'This is your mother, you need to handle it.' She genuinely liked Roberta and didn't want to have problems between them." And Roberta appeared to like Irene as well, at least as far as John could see.

On January 8, 1989, Jeremy John Barron was born. Both Irene and Jack were thrilled, as were doting grandparents Roberta Butler and Jack and Norma Paget.

A few months after Jeremy's birth, Jack, Irene and Jeremy moved south, back to Sacramento, where Jack found work once again in the supermarket business. Once more Denise rented a house for the three of them, and now infant Jeremy. From things Irene told her, Denise believed that the return to Sacramento was at Irene's insistence, because she was feuding with Dave and Patty over their influence on Jack; Irene believed that Dave and Patty were trying to break up her marriage with Jack, according to Denise.

By this time, Denise had begun dating an older man, Cliff Call, who was involved in a bitterly contested divorce that also involved ownership of a business Cliff operated. Often when Cliff came to pick Denise up, he and Jack would discuss the status of the case, and Cliff would fill Jack in on the woes of the long-running litigation.

On one occasion, Cliff was about at his wit's end.

"I told him I was fed up with all the hassles," Cliff recalled. "He laughed and said if it was him, he'd do away with her first." At the time, Cliff thought Jack was simply running his mouth; later, though, he wasn't so sure.

Ten

Denise also noticed a change in Jack's demeanor after the return to Sacramento.

"Jack was becoming more forceful," Denise recalled. "He was more controlling. Now she had to dress a certain way, or do things the way Jack wanted. It seemed to me that she just kind of lost some of the independence she'd gained after the divorce from Keith."

One of the aspects of Jack's behavior that began to irritate Denise was Jack's near-obsession with his appearance and cleanliness. At home, Jack constantly inspected himself in the mirror, and whenever he went out, he carried a clear plastic Ziploc bag with a cotton cloth.

"Every stoplight, every stop sign, Jack would be checking himself in the mirror. He'd take the cloth out of the bag, and wipe his face, his hair. He couldn't stand to have any perspiration on him."

Jack had other obsessions as well, Denise recalled.

"They'd get in the car to go somewhere," Denise said, "and Irene would get in, and Jack would lock her door. Then he'd get out of the car, check to make sure the garage was locked, then the windows, then the front door, then back to the garage, then back to the front door. Every time they went somewhere." It appeared to Denise that Jack had some sort of crazy obsession with locks.

And Jack began to display fits of childish temper, usually accompanied by slamming doors or throwing things.

"He had a little sports car," Denise said, "and once he and Irene were going to the store. They got in a minor fender bender on the way. There was hardly a little dent on the bumper, but it was like, for Jack, instant road rage.

"Jack gets out of the car and he just blows up. He throws his keys on the hood, scratching the paint. The damage from the keys was worse than the hit on the bumper. Forget about the shopping; he and Irene came back to the house, he comes stomping through the door, slamming it.

"I said, 'What's wrong? What happened to the store?' and he goes stomping off without answering. Irene said he had a little dent in his car."

Jack would lose his temper if the family room or the kitchen was the slightest bit messy, Denise recalled.

Irene took all this in stride according to Denise.

"She'd make jokes about it," Denise said. "She'd say, 'Before he gets up, I'd better clean this up so he doesn't get mad.' When Denise would persist in asking Irene why she allowed Jack to act this way, Irene would excuse her husband.

"She'd say, 'It's just Jack. It's just part of his personality. It has to do with his mom.' "

By the spring of 1989, Denise was ready to move in with Cliff. They purchased a new house that was under construction. One day while visiting Irene, Denise discovered some photographs of another house, also under construction.

What's this? Denise asked Irene.

Oh, Irene said, that's the house we've just bought.

Denise was amazed that Irene and Jack had kept secret the fact that they, too, were buying a house. It seemed, to Denise, unnatural.

"I mean, here we were both doing the same things, like picking carpets and tiles and that sort of thing, and she'd never said a word about it. I asked her why they hadn't told me, and Irene said, 'Jack didn't want you to know.' " So Irene hadn't even told her best friend, at her younger husband's insistence.

Just where Jack obtained the money to buy the house—as it turned out, the house on Southbreeze—wasn't clear to Denise and Cliff. They suspected that Roberta had provided the money, and that the reason Jack didn't want anyone to know about the house is that he did not want anyone to think that he was less of a man than Cliff, at least in having the money to buy a house.

John observed something a bit similar in Jack's behavior as well. He recalled visiting his sister and brother-in-law about the time they moved into the new house on Southbreeze, just after it was completed.

By this time, John had seen Jack Barron under a variety of circumstances, and, like Denise, some of John's initial acceptance of Jack was wearing off. To John, Jack seemed to be excessively self-centered, demanding. He was alternatively boastful and possessive, and could be quite confrontational if he didn't get what he thought he was entitled to.

"I'd always be taken aback by his childish ways," John recalled later. "I had seen one or more bouts of his temper, where somebody crossed him and he'd . . . if he was upset about something, he might stomp out of the house angrily, maybe slam the door . . .

"When they were moving into the house there on Southbreeze, here was a brand-new tract, some of the houses aren't even finished yet, but theirs is done. And there was a problem with the air-conditioning. And through the process of purchasing the house and being around, Jack learned who the people were, who the superintendent of the job was, who the honchos were, and we're there at the house, they've just moved in, the air-conditioning's not working right, it's supposed to be guaranteed or something.

"And Jack said, 'This is ridiculous, a brand-new house, and this isn't working. We'll see about this!' And he stomps out of the house and he goes looking for this guy, and gives him a piece of his mind, and demands that the guy be at the house to fix this by such and such a time, or else.

"So anytime Jack thought he had a right to something, or that he had been put upon, he'd be quick to rise to the occasion."

Sometimes John thought Jack was acting like this to show off for John's benefit. It was like Jack was insecure in himself, and needed to prove to John that he was capable of being a man, and taking care of John's little sister, even if she was four years older than Jack.

"It was like, 'I'm the man, I've got this new wife, who's older than me, but I'm the man, and I take care of things, I'm an in-charge guy,' " John said later.

On some extended family get-togethers, when Roberta was present, Roberta made every effort to cater to her son's needs and desires, John thought.

"I had a number of contacts with Roberta over the years," John said later, "and of course my parents saw quite a bit of her. What I saw of Roberta was this very doting, motherly type. She was this kind of take-control type, take over control of everything.

"You know, 'I know how to do it, I'll do it for you, you don't have to worry about a thing.' This was the type of woman she was. She never came into the house without an armful of groceries. Every time she came to visit. Because she just knew they weren't getting enough of the right food. She was going to make sure they had the right stuff in the house.

"She was always very gracious and accommodating, any time our side of the family was around. I mean, she'd wait on you hand and foot. She was continually in the kitchen, preparing food, doing the dishes. I'd go in, you know, after a meal and a visit, if she was around, and I'd go start to do dishes and she'd throw me out of the kitchen. She was going to take care of it. So that's the Roberta I knew.

"I can tell you that Jack and Irene and those two kids were her whole life. She lived for being around them, and doing for them. She would sacrifice herself to make sure they had what she thought they needed."

Years later, one of Roberta's best friends in Benicia agreed with John's perception of Roberta. Bea Kennedy, a young mother of three, recalled Roberta's joy at the marriage of Jack and Irene, and the prospects of their new family.

"She was happy, very happy," Bea recalled. "She knew he was going to be set from now on, and have a family. Her worries were over. Now she would have someone who would care for him the way she did. She always worried about him. She was very protective of him."

So protective of Jack, Bea thought later, that it was even to cost Roberta her life.

A bit more than nine months after Jack and Irene moved into the new house on Southbreeze, on March 28, 1990, Irene gave birth again, this time to a daughter, Ashley Ann.

Now the Barron family had two small children, only 15 months apart in age.

Meanwhile, Cliff's divorce had finally gone through, so he and Denise were married in the summer of 1989. A bit less than a year later, Denise gave birth to twins. Their house was about two minutes away from Jack and Irene's.

Now both of the high school friends had husbands, homes, and babies, just as they always wanted.

Denise and Irene kept in frequent contact, often shopping together, or taking the babies to the park. To Denise, it seemed that Irene felt perfectly comfortable in telling her things; it was only later that she began to wonder whether Irene had kept some of her dissatisfaction back. In any event, by the end of May, 1992, Irene called Denise and said she had to talk to her.

"I can still see her sitting on the deck," Denise recalled. "The kids were playing in the backyard. She told me that she thought Jack was having an affair."

Irene detailed the reasons for her suspicions to Denise. Jack had recently spent a weekend out of town with some train buffs, one of whom was a woman who worked at Jack's store. When Irene wanted Jack to give her a telephone number where he could be reached, Jack wouldn't do it.

"He said *he'd* call *her*," Denise said.

Irene said she was so upset about this possibility that she'd called Roberta, to ask her what she thought. Roberta had agreed with Irene that it certainly sounded suspicious, but it was impossible for Jack to be having an affair. Roberta told Irene that Jack would never do such a thing, not after Elmore.

Denise told Irene that she agreed with Roberta, but not for the same reasons.

"Jack isn't a good enough liar," Denise told Irene. "He just wouldn't be capable of that."

Not long after this conversation, Jack and Irene left the children with Roberta and went to Lake Tahoe with Patty and Dave.

When they returned, Denise asked Irene how the trip had been.

Irene seemed very happy, Denise thought.

"It was wonderful," Irene told her. "It was the honeymoon we never had."

Denise asked Irene if she'd confronted Jack with her suspicions.

She had, Irene said. But Jack had convinced her it was all in her imagination. He would never have an affair, he said.

Meanwhile, to the Pagets, it seemed Irene was at last in her element, taking care of her babies, cooking, and cleaning house, even if money was tight. Jack and Norma Paget sold their motor home and moved to an apartment in the Sacramento suburb of Citrus Heights, where they could see much more of Irene, Jack, and the babies, while John made it a practice to talk to Irene twice a month or so, long-distance.

"She didn't need a lot of expensive, material things to make her happy," John said. "She told me one time that she had everything she wanted. She had two beautiful children, a husband who loved her, who she loved. And she had a home and that was really all she needed.

"Irene, like all of us, had her moments when she didn't feel good or got upset about one thing or another. But she was not real vocal about it, and she was not a screamer. Or a big crier, or things of that nature. She would tend to keep it inside and somehow work through it. When I would call her on the phone, she would always be upbeat and happy and contented. Contentment is a word I think that really describes Irene at this stage of her life."

So, by early June of 1992, the Pagets had every reason to believe that Irene was happier than she'd ever been.

But that was when Jack called John on the morning of June 8, 1992, with terrible news.

Eleven

John was in his office in Fallbrook when his secretary paged him.

"Your brother-in-law Jack is on the phone," the secretary told John.

John picked up the telephone.

"Hi, Jack, how are you doing?" John asked.

There was a short pause.

"Well, John, I've got some bad news," Jack said.

"What's the matter?"

"Irene's dead."

At first John heard it, then he didn't hear it. It didn't register.

"What do you mean, Irene is dead?" John asked.

"I don't know, Irene's dead," Jack said. "You've got to get here."

Jack broke down and started crying.

Somehow John discovered from Jack that Irene had been found dead in her bed, and that the police were at the scene.

"My first thought was," John said later, "what happened? Did someone come in in the middle of the night and murder her? Was there some robbery at the house? What took place? Why were the police there? But right away I was in the mindset that she'd been murdered."

Jack couldn't or wouldn't give John any details. John kept pressing him, but Jack could offer nothing to explain this frightful news.

"I don't know," Jack said, over and over. "They won't tell me anything." Jack said the police had cordoned off the house and were refusing to let him in.

John wanted to know whether Jack had told Jack and Norma Paget. Jack said he'd called them and told them to come over, that something had happened, but he hadn't told them exactly what.

John put the telephone down and told his secretary to get him the first plane to Sacramento.

In a daze John rushed home and threw some clothes into a bag, then rushed to the airport. By the time he reached the Sacramento airport it was about 3 P.M. Jack and Norma picked him up. By that time they'd been to the house on Southbreeze and had learned the awful truth.

Denise was at her house when Jack called her. She'd just put the twins down for a nap.

"I thought it was Irene, because we always talked about that time of the morning. I picked up the phone and it was Jack," Denise remembered. A stilted conversation ensued.

"Denise, are you sitting down?" Jack asked.

Denise sat down, wondering what silly game Jack was playing now.

"Okay," said Denise, "I'm sitting."

"She's gone," Jack said.

"Gone? Who's gone?"

"Irene's gone."

"Gone where?"

"She's dead," Jack said.

Denise screamed. She stood up, firing questions at Jack. For some reason, like John Paget, Denise immediately assumed that Irene had been murdered; she thought Jack was telling her someone had broken into the house.

"I'll be there in a minute," she told Jack, and gathering

up her twins, immediately rushed over to Christina Hamilton's house with Cliff.

When the Calls arrived, Jack and Norma Paget were already there. John Paget had not yet arrived, nor had Roberta Butler and her boyfriend, Tim O'Keefe.

A Sheriff's detective was in the house, but seems to have said little to anyone, or indeed, made any sort of impression on Denise.

"We sat there for awhile, and Jack tried to tell us what happened, how Christina had found Irene. About Jeremy letting Christina in. He said they didn't know what it was, but that they had told him it didn't look like a burglary. He said they said there were no signs of a struggle. He said it didn't look like she was suffocated."

Jack's use of the word "suffocated" in this situation was possibly meaningful—almost as if he were taking pains to assure Irene's friends and family that such a thing could not have happened, and attributing this to the police. Just how Jack would know this, however, is unclear, since at that point the autopsy had not been conducted, and the police had not formed any conclusions. Moreover, with the pillow found over Irene's face, there was at least *some* evidence of suffocation.

At one point that morning, Cliff Call was overcome by his emotions, and burst into tears. He put his head on Jack's shoulder and said, "Jack, I'm so sorry."

Jack pushed Cliff away and looked at him as if he'd lost his mind.

"Right then and there," Cliff said later, "the thought struck me that maybe Jack had something to do with this. He was so unemotional about the whole thing."

Twelve

Not so the Pagets, however.

After picking up John at the airport, the three Pagets drove without words through the city to the Southbreeze house, Norma sobbing most of the way. They arrived just about the time Schmunk was finishing his autopsy on Irene Barron and failing to determine the cause of her death.

By the time the Pagets arrived back at the Southbreeze house, Roberta was there, along with her boyfriend, Tim O'Keefe, as well as Denise and Cliff. The police had by now turned the house back over to Jack.

When the Pagets entered, John wanted to talk to Jack as soon as possible.

All the way north on the plane, John's mind had been reeling.

"All these thoughts were rushing through my mind, while I tried to figure out whatever had possibly happened," John recalled. "I kept thinking *my poor sister has been killed.* I mean, in my own mind I had already come to the assumption there was a murder."

So John wanted to find out from Jack just exactly what happened, and what the police had told him.

"Where's Jack?" John asked, and someone pointed at

the rear bedroom, the one where Christina Hamilton had found Irene dead early that same morning. John knocked on the door and entered.

Jack was sitting on the bed with his head in his hands. John sat down next to him and put his arm around Jack's shoulders.

It seemed to John that Jack was devastated by Irene's death. He was still weeping. John tried to console him. Mostly, however, he wanted information from Jack.

"What happened?" John persisted.

Jack again said he didn't know what happened to Irene or how she died. Jack again told the story of Christina Hamilton's discovery of Irene's body.

Jack told John that the Coroner's Office had taken Irene's body to the morgue, where an autopsy would be performed to find out how she died. By this time, John already knew that Irene hadn't been shot, stabbed or strangled, as he had first feared; and that it was possible that Irene had died of natural causes.

As the afternoon progressed, others dropped by to give their sympathies to Jack and the Pagets. One was Father Duggan, the parish priest at St. Paul's Catholic Church, in Florin. The way Father Duggan consoled Jack and the Pagets, and from what he said of Irene, John realized that Irene had been at least attending the Roman Catholic services.

That's odd, John thought, *she never told me that*. But John concluded that maybe Father Duggan was just being polite. But two days later, at the funeral service, John was to realize that Irene had become a committed Catholic, and concluded that she had done so to satisfy Roberta's anxiety about the upbringing of Jeremy and Ashley.

Later, John was to come to believe that after her divorce from Keith, Irene would have done almost anything to maintain her marriage with Jack, even to the point of adopting a religion she was unfamiliar with.

"I think it's more likely that it was Roberta's influence,"

John said later, "because Roberta was the staunch Catholic. Irene's nature is, she's very serious about her marriage, she's already had one failed marriage, she wants this one to work. Which is, I think, why she never confided to me that she'd had problems with Jack, or told me that she'd decided to become a Catholic."

It was, in a sense, evidence of Irene's commitment to her marriage and her children.

In any event, arrangements had to be made for the funeral, which would be held at St. Paul's as soon as the Coroner's Office released Irene's body.

That happened the following morning, Tuesday. But when the Pagets asked the Coroner's Office if they had been able to determine why Irene died, they were informed that the determination was still under consideration by the pathologist, Dr. Schmunk.

On the same day, John went with Jack to the funeral home to make the arrangements.

"I remember being in the funeral director's office," John recalled, "and talking about the selection of the casket. I know these things are practical realities of life that have to be dealt with, but the funeral director's sitting there and he's suggesting [to Jack] that you might want to get a double plot, because it's cheaper to buy two now, than buy two separately. And Jack decides, yeah, he thinks he's going to go ahead and do that, buy a double plot.

"Now, this is my first time of ever arranging a funeral for anybody. I had no idea of what's involved. And a double plot like that, it's piggy-back. They bury Irene 12 feet down and then you know, they go six feet down with the one on top."

John thought Jack was being foolish.

"You know, Jack," John said at the time, "you're a young man. This is ridiculous. You don't need to buy a double plot. You're likely going to remarry someday. And then what are you going to do, be buried next to your first wife? After you've been married to your second wife for 35 or 40 years? It makes no sense. It's going to go over someday like a lead balloon with your new wife. Why don't you save yourself a few bucks and let's just forget about this?''

But Jack thought the double plot option was an excellent idea.

''He wanted to be buried there with his wife,'' John recalled, even if it didn't happen for another 40 years.

The following day, both Jack and John went back to the funeral home to complete the arrangements. The main question was whether the casket should be open or closed. Denise Call, for one, strongly wanted the casket to be open, because she wanted to see her friend one last time.

By then, the two other Paget children, Paul and Debra, had arrived in Sacramento with their own families. As a result, John, Debbie and Paul all went with Jack to the funeral home. So did Roberta and Tim O'Keefe.

''This was the viewing of Irene's body,'' John recalled. ''There was a—because of the autopsy, and because of the trauma to the body, and the period of time that had elapsed, there was concern as to whether this would be open casket or closed casket.

''And Jack kept insisting he wanted it to be an open casket ceremony. And I and my sister and several others said, this is really not what we want. But Jack's—we thought, we've got to do it Jack's way. So Jack asked me to go to the viewing with him to see if Irene looked good enough to be displayed.''

Even more than five years later, John Paget's emotion from the scene that was about to unfold was still evident, even if it is hard to describe in printed words.

''So we go to the funeral home on Wednesday,'' John recalled, his voice breaking. ''The funeral director tried to explain or warn us.

''He said, 'She looks really good, but she may not look the way you remember her.' And Jack wanted to go in by himself. But Roberta wouldn't have any part of it. She in-sisted that she be there. So she went in with him. And then they spent a short time in there and came back out in tears.

"And so my sister and my brother and I went in. And of course this is—I had just seen my sister for the last time alive, only a few months before. So we walked in and she was laying there. And it was obvious who it was, I mean, I could identify and recognize, This is my sister. She's—This smack of reality hits you right in the face.

"Because from Monday until Thursday you intellectu-ally know that she's gone, you intellectually know that she's at the funeral home. You know that she's undergone this autopsy. But you're never prepared for your own fam-ily member, as to what the reality is until you walk up to that casket and she's laying there.

"And she was swollen . . ."

At this point, even five years later, John began to cry.

"I'm sorry," he said, in an interview, and then contin-ued, slowly. "I bent down to kiss her on the cheek," he said, his voice breaking once again and turning to a whis-per, ". . . and she was ice-cold."

"So anyway," John continued, later, "we walked out after a few minutes. And we all agreed we would close the cas-ket. We didn't want the rest of the family to see her. I told Jack: I do not want my parents to be subjected to this. It's cruel."

The casket remained closed.

A day later, Irene was laid to rest in the double plot at St. Mary's Cemetery in Sacramento. Isn't that something, John thought, numb, as they drove through the gates for the final farewell to Irene. Born at St. Mary's Hospital in Reno; buried at St. Mary's Cemetery in Sacramento.

SACRAMENTO

July–November, 1992

Thirteen

After funeral services at St. Paul's and St. Mary's, the Paget families returned to their own homes, still perplexed as to the cause of Irene's death. Roberta, however, stayed on for a few days at the Southbreeze house. She helped Jack sort through all of Irene's things. Some were thrown out, others were set aside to be offered at garage sales, and others, more personal items, were boxed up and put in the garage. Jack planted a tree in tribute to Irene, but that was the extent of any material effort to maintain her memory.

It was as if, for Jack and the kids, that Irene had never existed. That was the way both Jack and Roberta were, some thought: once a person was gone, they were gone, so there was no point to hanging onto the past, whether they were named Elmore or even Irene.

One other who could not put Irene's death away was Dr. Schmunk of the Sacramento Coroner's Office. He continued to puzzle over his findings, or rather, lack of them. Just like the bewildered Pagets and Denise Call, Schmunk wanted to know what killed Irene; the difference between them, though, was that he was the one who was being paid to find out.

What could have caused Irene to die? Was it a reaction to some sort of medication? Irene had been menstruating at the time of her death, and was wearing a tampon. Schmunk was aware of previously recorded cases of toxic shock syndrome related to tampons. Samples of Irene's tissues were sent to a consulting laboratory in the hope of finding something that might explain her sudden, unexpected demise. Outside of minor bacteriological infection consistent with the reports that Irene had been suffering from a cold at the time of her death, nothing unusual turned up.

As for other potential toxins, a sample of Irene's blood was examined by Sacramento County Laboratory of Forensic Services—in other words, the crime lab. The blood sample was negative for any trace of barbiturates, hypnotics, anti-depressants, opiates, cocaine, cyanide, or any other type of poison.

Well, if Irene hadn't reacted to some sort of medicine, poison, or toxin, what accounted for her slurring of speech?

In mid-June, after Irene's funeral, Schmunk called in a consulting neuropathologist, Dr. Surl L. Nielsen. Nielsen examined Irene's brain. He found some evidence of hemorrhage deep within the brain, and a slightly enlarged pineal gland.

The pineal gland is one of the least-understood portions of the brain's anatomy. The gland is connected to the eyes, and it appears to operate almost as a sort of light meter inside the brain. Based on the intensity of light entering the eyes, the pineal gland manufactures and releases greater or lesser levels of melatonin, a hormone which regulates other bodily functions, such as the adrenal glands, the sex organs and the thyroid. Irene's pineal gland was the site of a number of cysts—in other words, growths inside the brain.

This could explain several things. The slurring of words, for one. Such cysts, in Nielsen's experience, could cause headaches, staggering, or slurring. As the cysts grow, these effects become progressively worse. But none of this happens overnight. In fact, Nielsen believed that Irene had these brain cysts for a number of years. Such cysts could cause death if they grew to the point where they interfered with the flow of spinal fluid to and from the brain; in that case, the backed-up fluid inside the brain would cause a rupture, which would lead to death; but usually, if the cyst was that advanced, a person would have sought treatment for it long before; and in any case, Irene's condition was far from that advanced.

However, because the pineal gland is affected by light, it was possible that Irene, in pain from the light, had pulled the pillow over her face to shut out the light, exactly as Schmunk himself had suggested.

Schmunk next obtained Irene's medical records from Kaiser Permanente Hospital; these were of no help, because as far as her own doctors knew, Irene Barron had been perfectly healthy up to the day she died.

As July turned into August, Schmunk considered several other alternatives. Perhaps Irene had died of some mysterious, fast-acting disease that left no trace behind in her system; or perhaps she had been subjected to some unknown toxin, one that the lab hadn't been able to isolate.

It was also true, Schmunk conceded, that Irene might have been asphyxiated, but that left the question: who did it?

And the evidence of such a crime was, in Schmunk's view, far too thin to state unequivocally that Irene had been murdered. If he were forced to testify, Schmunk knew, he would be eviscerated by any competent defense lawyer, because he would never be able to say for sure what had caused Irene to die.

While Schmunk was mulling all this over, the Pagets were growing extremely frustrated. Despite the fact that many days had gone by, still the Coroner's Office refused to issue its report on Irene's death.

John Paget had the impression that most autopsy reports took around a month to complete.

"We called the Coroner's Office requesting a copy of the autopsy report, and each time we would request it, they would indicate they hadn't completed it yet," John recalled.

"We were so anxious to find out what caused her death, because at that point we were thinking, well, maybe she had an aneurism, or a heart attack, or any number of possibilities, for natural death."

Despite John's initial instinct that Irene had somehow been murdered, no one, either in the Coroner's Office or the Sheriff's Department, ever indicated that anyone had ever even considered the possibility of foul play.

Irene's death was simply a big mystery to the Pagets, who couldn't help but feel that if they only knew why Irene had died, they could begin to accept it and go on with their lives.

"So we were anxious to get the report, and we kept calling and calling and calling," John recalled, "asking, 'Where is this report?' Because I was always under the impression that an autopsy report seemed like it took 30 or 45 days."

But despite all the calls, according to John, the Coroner's Office kept insisting that the report had not been completed yet, all the way up to November of that year.

In fact, however, in the middle of August, even while the Pagets were being told something quite different, Schmunk issued his final autopsy report and the asserted cause of death.

"No evidence of trauma," Schmunk wrote. "Cause of death undetermined . . ."

Fourteen

By the time Schmunk issued his final report, no one in the Sacramento Sheriff's Department was paying any attention to Jack. Jack had returned to the Southbreeze house, and resumed his regular night shift at Lucky's.

The Pagets, the Calls, the Southbreeze neighbors, members of the church, and Jack's friends and co-workers all rallied to support Jack and the children after their loss. Some brought food; others brought money, in the form of checks tucked away inside cards of consolation. At least one thing was true as never before when Irene was alive: Jack was the center of everyone's attention and solicitude.

At one point, Denise Call and Jack's sister-in-law Debra Harris suggested to Jack and Roberta that Jeremy and Ashley go back to New Jersey with Debra for awhile to give Jack a chance to cope with things. But Jack and Roberta thought it would be harder for the children to be away from their father after losing their mother.

Still, everyone was eager to help Jack in any way they could.

"When Irene died," John Paget recalled, "the entire family, as families typically do, saw this young man with two children to raise on his own. We knew that he worked at Lucky's as a stocking clerk. We knew that he didn't make a tremendous amount of money. And everybody came forward with hundred-dollar gifts, five-hundred-dollar gifts. All this cash that he got at the funeral.''

John thought Jack was appreciative of everyone's support. But John wanted to do more. He pulled Jack aside after the funeral.

"I know things are going to be tight for you a little bit,'' John told his brother-in-law. "I want to help you out. I will send you a hundred dollars a month, just to help support Ashley and Jeremy. This money's for the kids, to buy them clothes, whatever they need.'' Jack was very grateful for his help, John thought.

Along with disposing of Irene's things after the funeral, Jack had made a number of other changes in his life in the following month. One of the most important resulted in an expansion of the population at the Southbreeze house. Sometime in July, Jack decided to take in someone he referred to as a "roommate."

At least, that's what he called the new arrival in telling the Paget family about his new domestic arrangements.

The "roommate" was Starla Hayes, a delicatessen clerk at Lucky's Supermarket, who had been an acquaintance of Jack's for some time. Some of Jack and Starla's co-workers, in fact, thought Jack and Starla were more than just good friends.

Indeed, it turned out that on the night when Irene lay dead in the rear bedroom of the Southbreeze house, Jack and Starla had been together—not at work, but at the Kaiser Hospital. Starla had begun feeling sick at work, so Jack had driven her to the hospital, where Starla was found to be suffering from some sort of hemorrhage. Jack waited at the hospital until Starla's condition was stabilized. He had been returning from having driven Starla to her own home on the morning that Irene's body was discovered.

Starla's own marriage had recently hit a rocky spot. In

the aftermath of Irene's death, Jack's suggestion of sharing the Southbreeze house seemed to make a sort of sense: Jack had room at the house, and Starla needed a place to stay for herself and her children. It was crowded, but it helped financially and in terms of child care for work schedules.

But when John Paget heard of this arrangement, a small warning bell went off inside his brain. John thought it was odd that Jack would take in a female "roommate" so soon after Irene's death. Even the word "roommate" sounded suspicious to John. He found himself wondering whether Jack had begun an affair with Starla before Irene's death. Those thoughts led John inevitably to the unthinkable: if his brother-in-law had replaced Irene so quickly, who was to say Jack hadn't planned to do so all along?

Which in turn meant that Jack would know a lot more about Irene's death than anyone suspected . . .

But voicing such suspicions hardly seemed appropriate under the circumstances, John thought. His parents, Jack and Norma, were still trying to come to grips with their own grief over Irene's death. To suggest to them that the father of their two grandchildren might be a murderer would not only be highly premature, but it might also be unspeakably cruel. So John tried to shove the suspicion out of his mind, and kept his own counsel; but from that point forward, it was inevitable that John would begin seeing Jack with an ever more critical eye.

Unbeknownst to John Paget, by this time Cliff and Denise Call had been talking about Jack's behavior, along with his remark a few years earlier about "doing her in" before going through a divorce. The scene in Christina Hamilton's living room had stuck with Cliff, as well.

"I said, 'Denise, you don't want to rule this out. Maybe you ought to think about Jack being the culprit here.' "

Denise wouldn't have it.

"I didn't want to think somebody I knew, that I let into my life, that he could be capable of doing something like that," Denise said later. It seemed absolutely impossible.

*   *   *

In later years, one of the aspects of Jack's behavior that attracted the most comment was his apparent fetish over cleanliness, as Denise had noted long before. His own father, Elmore—though he admitted not having seen "Jackie" more than three times in 20 years—compared Jack's phobia about dirt and disorder to Howard Hughes' well-known pathological anxiety over germs.

In fact, Jack was so "fastidious"—to use Elmore's word—that he constantly patrolled his own house with a damp cloth wiping things down. Or, if Irene had vacuumed, Jack was said to follow along behind her, wiping out the tracks the machine had made in the carpet.

However, as anyone who ever had to take care of two small children knows, it's virtually impossible to keep everything clean and neat all the time. Kids are messy, and everyone knows it. Still, as Denise had observed, this appears to have been at least one of the areas of disputation between Jack and Irene, before her death; Jack constantly complained that Irene wasn't keeping the house neat enough for his standards; and poor Irene, desperate to prove that she could be a good wife and mother, strove valiantly to keep up with Jack's seemingly obsessive cleanliness demands.

Now, with Irene out and Starla in, some of the same idiosyncrasies began cropping up between Jack and Starla.

Starla, however, appears to have been made of different stuff than Irene. While she may have felt the Jack she knew at work to be good-looking in a certain sort of way, and sometimes even witty, the closeup picture was a different story.

Apart from the constant cleaning and the wiping out of the vacuum cleaner tracks, the main problem seems to have been over Starla's children. The fact was, Jack wasn't very good with Starla's kids, at least in Starla's view. He simply didn't know how to handle them. Nor were Starla's chil-

dren any too happy to be taking orders from the big lug
who wasn't their real father.

All of this tension—between Jack and Starla, and
Starla's kids and Jack—soon began to spill over into Jack's
relationship with his own children: little Jeremy, then almost four, and Ashley, just two-and-a-half.

One afternoon in November, while Jack was trying to
get some sleep before having to go off to work his midnight
shift at the supermarket, Jeremy was feeling particularly out
of sorts. Suffering from a head cold and general dissatisfaction, Jeremy kept demanding attention from Jack. He
cried and cried.

"I want my mommy," Jeremy told Jack, over and over
again. At one point Jeremy went into the bedroom and began kicking and screaming, then knocking his head against
the wall, crying, "Mommy, Mommy, Mommy," over and
over again.

Finally Jack, exasperated with the child, exploded at Jeremy, according to Starla. He spanked Jeremy and yelled at
him.

"If you don't keep quiet and get to sleep, I'll make sure
you go where your mother is," Jack told Jeremy.

Later, Starla was to consider this merely an intemperate
outburst by Jack, the sort of thing one might say (and later
deeply regret) when one is feeling harried. In any event,
Jeremy eventually quieted down, Jack got some sleep, and
later that night, went off to work.

But the whole aspect of Jack's relationship with the children seemed uncomfortable to Starla. It was as if Jack
couldn't handle it when the children didn't do exactly as
he wanted them to; in another way, it seemed that the children were, to Jack, more like obstacles or problems to be
dealt with rather than real people.

Not long after this incident involving Jeremy, Starla
moved out.

SACRAMENTO
Sunday, February 7, 1993

Fifteen

Little Jeremy was deeply unhappy. He still missed his mother. Normally, the towheaded Jeremy was of a sunny disposition, smiling a lot. But since the death of Irene, and the changes associated with Starla's arrival and departure, Jeremy had slid into a funk. His mood was made worse by a persistent cold.

By Sunday morning, February 7, Jeremy's cold had developed into a deep congestion, accompanied by a persistent coughing that came close to retching. Jack gave Jeremy a dose of cough syrup in the morning, and a second dose some time later. Jack then put Jeremy to bed.

About 12:45 in the afternoon, a baby-sitter, 17-year-old Jennifer Walters, arrived at the Southbreeze house preparatory to a baby-sitting assignment from Jack that was to begin at 1 P.M. She knocked on the door several times, but there was no answer. Jennifer then rang the doorbell, but still no one came to the door. Later, Jennifer was to estimate that she'd stayed as long as ten minutes at the front door of the Southbreeze house waiting for someone to admit her. Eventually Jennifer left and returned to her own house. She called the Barron residence to see if Jack still wanted her to sit with the two children.

Jack answered the telephone. When Jennifer explained that she'd arrived just before one and knocked but no one appeared to be home, Jack told her that he must have been in the shower. Jack told her he still needed her to sit, so Jennifer returned to the Southbreeze house.

This time Jack was there to admit her. Jack told Jennifer that both of the children were asleep. They looked in on both of the children, who appeared to be sleeping. Jeremy was lying on his right side with his face toward the bedroom wall.

Jack told Jennifer that he was going to take a nap before getting ready to go to work. He told Jennifer not to let the children sleep more than three hours. Jack then went to bed.

About two-forty, Ashley woke up. Jennifer spent a few minutes with Ashley, then decided to go check on Jeremy.

Jennifer knew almost immediately that something was wrong. To Jennifer, Jeremy lay in exactly the same position that he'd been in when she had seen him shortly after her arrival. It appeared to Jennifer that Jeremy hadn't moved an inch.

Jennifer tried to wake Jeremy up, but Jeremy seemed lifeless. Jennifer later recalled that at that point her mind seemed to go blank. She ran to Jack's room and got him awake, then ran to the telephone to call 911. She yelled to Jack that the 911 dispatcher said they should start CPR.

But Jack wouldn't do it.

"Don't bother," he said, bending over Jeremy. "It's too late anyway."

About five minutes after three, the EMTs from the Florin Fire District arrived at the Southbreeze house. When EMT Aaron Webster arrived he saw Jeremy lying on the living room floor. Jack was sitting on the living room couch, holding Ashley. The leader of the EMT team told Webster to escort Jack, Ashley, and Jennifer out of the room while the rest of the team worked to revive Jeremy.

The EMTs bent over Jeremy, but they could detect no pulse. Nor was Jeremy breathing. The EMTs attempted to revive Jeremy by starting cardiopulmonary resuscitation. They inserted a tube down his throat and secured it with tape, and inserted a needle in his neck coupled to an IV bag of salt solution. They affixed a number of EKG pads to his chest and upper limbs, then quickly bundled him up and raced for the hospital.

Although it was obvious that Jeremy was dead, the emergency medical people always went through this procedure when a child was involved—to spare the feelings of the family.

Meanwhile, Webster asked for details from Jack. Jack told Webster that Jeremy had been suffering from a bad cold, and that he'd given Jeremy some cough syrup. Jack told Webster that he'd been asleep when Jeremy was discovered by the baby-sitter. Jack added that his wife, Jeremy's mother, had died the year before.

Later, John Paget was unable to recall how he found out that his four-year-old nephew was dead.

"Obviously, somebody must have called," John said, but the details of who and how were gone, repressed by the horror of it. He did know it wasn't Jack, however.

Denise Call, on the other hand, remembered the day vividly. Jack called her. By this time the Calls had moved to Vancouver, Washington, where Jack tracked her down.

In a scene out of a repeating dream, he began:

"Denise, are you sitting down?"

Denise knew this time that there was no joke.

"Jeremy's gone," Jack said, and Denise knew exactly what Jack meant.

This time she yelled at Jack.

"How can this be? How can two people die for no reason?" Denise demanded.

Jack told her that he had no idea. He said the coroner's office was investigating. He had been asleep, Jack said, and Jeremy had been discovered by the baby-sitter.

Afterward, Denise and Cliff discussed the situation, and

this time Denise began to wonder whether Cliff had been right about Jack.

Again the Pagets assembled at the Southbreeze house, along with Roberta, Tim O'Keefe, Dave and Patty, and the others. Cliff and Denise, however, did not come.

This time the families' concerns were, if anything, even worse than with Irene. The unexplained death of a small child hung over them like something from a horrible dream, made the worse by the seeming inexplicability of it all.

After months of pestering the Coroner's Office, the Pagets had finally succeeding in prying loose a copy of Schmunk's autopsy report on Irene, however unenlightening it was. During those anxious months the family had speculated that perhaps Irene had died of an aneurism or heart attack, or at least some form of natural cause. But Schmunk's autopsy, with its cause undetermined, was of no help.

Now Jeremy was dead and the family was forced to worry: was there some sort of predisposition in either the Paget or Barron genes that might account for these sudden, medically undetermined deaths?

Or perhaps there was something in the soil under the Barron house—some sort of hidden toxic waste, like Love Canal in New York. Or maybe there was something wrong with the cough syrup Jack had given Jeremy—some sort of product tampering, like with the notorious Tylenol case some years before.

But there were no answers immediately forthcoming, and the mystery seemed no closer to being resolved.

Again there were the services at St. Paul's, with Father Duggan; again, the trip through St. Mary's gates, and another gathering around the gravesite, with its suddenly-needed double plot.

Once more Jack received cash-stuffed cards of condolence from his friends and relatives, meals from the neighbors, and the deepest sympathies of his co-workers.

For John Paget, however, the seeds of suspicion that had first sprouted the summer before were now spreading.

For one thing, to John, at least, Jack seemed to have perfected his role as the grieving man of the hour. It all seemed a little too practiced, too smooth, to John. Jack accepted the condolences as if he were the center of attention, John thought, sort of like a king accepting his due from his subjects, or perhaps an actor taking bows at the cast party after the show.

It irritated John: that was it, it was almost like a party atmosphere, he thought. Jack never cried at Jeremy's funeral, or even when they had lowered him into the ground. And the double plot: suddenly, to John, Jack's insistence on getting the double plot the year before seemed sinister.

Even before Jeremy's death, John had been aware of a budding irritation with his brother-in-law. It had started with the "roommate" business, but it ran deeper. As he had promised, John sent $100 a month to Jack to help support Irene's children. John was under the impression that Jack was having a hard time making ends meet financially.

But then, after Jeremy died, John prepared Jack's tax return for 1992.

"I'd always done Irene and Jack's tax returns," John said, later. "And through doing Jack's tax return [that years], it must have been in March of 1993, I learned how much money he really was getting from these different sources. And I said, 'What kind of an idiot am I? He doesn't need this money.' So I stopped paying him."

In fact, when John stopped to think about it, that's what he really thought of Jack: that Jack was a taker, taking, taking, always taking, but never giving.

In addition to his pay at the supermarket, Jack was also receiving assistance from Social Security due to Irene's death. Besides that, Jack had collected a $10,000 life insurance death benefit on Irene on July 13, 1992, and an additional $5,000 in November.

So by March, John decided he just wasn't going to send Jack any more money.

"After the check didn't come at its normal time," John recalled, "Jack got on the phone and called me. He said, 'I just wanted to let you know that I hadn't received your check this month. I just wondered if maybe it got lost in the mail.' He'd missed the check. This was maybe two weeks after I normally sent the money, around the first of the month. So I made an excuse, and told him I was a little short right now, that we might have to delay it a while. We just let it go at that."

Inside, however, John was steamed. *This guy is just taking advantage of my generosity,* John thought to himself. *Even with an expectation of it now, for it to come, when it doesn't show up on time, he's going to call up and remind me. So this is the kind of guy Jack is. I mean, he's a taker. From the get-go.*

What John did not then know was that Jack wouldn't miss the money: he was about to receive another $13,077.88, the death benefit for the life of Jeremy John Barron.

And after that check came, Jack planted a second tree next to the one commemorating Irene, and put all of Jeremy's clothes and toys on offer at a garage sale.

Sixteen

Even before Jeremy Barron went to where his mother was, his remains followed almost the same path as Irene. That is, they went to the Coroner's Office at 44 R Street, where, by the luck of the draw, the pathologist assigned to the case was none other than Dr. Gregory Schmunk.

In retrospect it appears that if Schmunk was genuinely baffled by Irene's death, he was even more so by Jeremy's. He began the autopsy of the three-foot-tall, 45-pound, four-year-old at 20 minutes after eight the day after Jeremy died.

First Schmunk inspected the body. He noted a purplish-red mottling along the right portion of the face, along with a single petechial hemorrhage in Jeremy's lower right eyelid.

Once again, Schmunk began the gruesome process of dismantling a human body—in this case, that of a four-year-old boy.

By the time it was over, Schmunk was where he had been with Irene Barron—stumped.

Looking back, based on interviews with a variety of officials of the Sacramento County Coroner's Office, the Sheriff's Department, and the Paget family, it appears that

Schmunk's bafflement was in large part due to his belief that there had to be some discernible natural or man-made illness that had caused the deaths of both Irene and Jeremy Barron.

It does not appear that Schmunk ever entertained any suspicions that Jeremy's death might be other than by natural causes. Unlike the case of Irene, no police agency was even notified of Jeremy's demise, although the case was briefly discussed at the county's multi-agency Child Death Review Committee. That committee included a representative from the Sheriff's Department and was chaired by Deputy District Attorney Robin Shakely, who was normally attached to that office's homicide unit.

In an interview years later, Shakely said she could recall that Jeremy's case was discussed at the committee, along with the information that Irene had died the year before. But it was her recollection that there was no indication of foul play, and that Schmunk was of the opinion that the cause of both deaths would be found to be natural, if only he could find the key.

To that end, Schmunk requested that a Coroner's deputy obtain all the over-the-counter and other medications present in the Southbreeze house for testing. He also obtained all of Jeremy's previous medical records in the hope that something, somewhere, would give him an idea of what to look for. Thus, Schmunk set off in search of a medical mystery, a search that was to last until well into the month of August of 1993.

With the death of Jeremy and the now-familiar lack of information about what might have caused it, the Pagets began to wonder whether they themselves were at risk from some hitherto undiagnosed malady. With first Irene dead, and now Jeremy, the lack of any clarity as to what had caused either of them to die had thrust all of the Pagets into a nightmarish world of all possibilities—made by far the worse by the fact that no one seemed to be able to say where the doctors should start looking.

By the late summer of 1993, after Schmunk issued his latest "undetermined" report on Jeremy's death, the Paget family decided to subject itself to medical testing. In New Jersey, Debra Harris put herself through a stress test for her heart to see if there were any abnormalities; there was nothing wrong. Both Jack and Norma Paget wore heart monitors for 24 hours. Norma's heart was fine, but Jack Paget's test indicated there might be some problem. But after further testing, it appeared that Jack Paget was completely normal as well.

Meanwhile, the Barron family pediatrician, Dr. William Coop, had already decided to begin some special testing on Ashley Barron. From his own review of his records on Jeremy, Coop could not identify a single possible cause for Jeremy's death; to Coop, Jeremy was a completely healthy, normal four-year-old boy. But the deaths of Irene and Jeremy prompted special caution in the case of Ashley.

Coop began with a test for sleep apnea—a phenomenon in which a person's breathing might suddenly stop during sleep.

Coop thought that if either Irene or Jeremy had suffered from sleep apnea, there might be a hereditary cause that had escaped Schmunk's detection. One way to verify that hypothesis was to subject three-year-old Ashley to a test called a sleep apnea oximetry screen. The idea was to measure the amount of oxygen taken in by Ashley during the course of breathing.

Based on the results of this screening, a second, more definitive test, a polysomnogram, was scheduled. This involved a sort of harness wrapped around Ashley's upper torso, which in turn was wired to sensors designed to detect Ashley's breathing characteristics—how often, how deep, how shallow, that sort of thing. The idea was to monitor Ashley while she was both asleep and awake to see whether there was any evidence of severe breathing disruptions during sleep. The information was recorded on a computer disk.

The overnight test was conducted on May 25, 1993, and the disk was then sent to a company in Cincinnati for processing. The following month, a pediatric neurologist, Dr. Carter Mosher, interpreted the results of the test.

To Mosher, it appeared that Ashley had experienced "abnormal overnight polysomnograms showing an apnea index of eight mainly due to central type apneas," or so he indicated in his written report to Coop.

Translated, this meant that Ashley was indeed experiencing periodic interruptions of her breathing while asleep.

Coop was unconvinced, particularly when Mosher acknowledged that he was not that familiar with the somnogram test, and particularly with tests involving children as young as Ashley.

Coop now took Ashley's test results and showed them to a pulmonary specialist, Dr. Albin Leon. Leon looked at the test results and opined that they were within normal limits. But, said Leon, one of the problems with the test was that it was not designed for use with small children—primarily because the harness was too loose. That in turn might mean there were false positives.

Following this test, another of Coop's colleagues at the hospital outfitted Ashley with a 24-hour heart monitor, similar to those worn by Jack and Norma Paget. This device was intended to record Ashley's heartbeat to see if there were any heart irregularities.

Coop tried to impress on Jack, he said later, the importance of getting Ashley to wear the heart halter for a long enough period to obtain results. But the test never was performed adequately, because Ashley didn't like wearing the halter. According to Coop, he tried to convince Jack to make Ashley complete the test, but he failed. Jack told Coop, Coop said later, that he was too busy.

*   *   *

Throughout that summer of testing for Ashley and the Pagets, both Roberta Butler's and Jack and Norma's anxiety about Ashley's health rose dramatically.

Outwardly, Ashley appeared to be a normal, healthy three-year-old. John Paget recalled her as a particularly outgoing and happy child.

Often Jack would take Ashley for extended visits to Roberta's or Jack and Norma's. Both sides of the family watched Ashley carefully for any sign of illness. Other than the normal colds and fevers experienced by any three-year-old, Ashley seemed perfectly healthy.

"We watched that girl like a hawk," Jack Paget was to say later, particularly when she was in bed.

Just what Ashley must have made of the traumatic events that had accompanied her first three years of existence is hard to say. Neither she nor Jack talked very much of Irene or Jeremy, at least while they were around the elder Pagets. Once, when looking at family photographs, Ashley saw a picture of Irene.

"Is that my mommy?" she asked. So dim was Ashley's memory of her mother that she wasn't sure. It was enough to make Norma's heart break.

As the summer of 1993 turned into the fall, and still no definitive answers about the deaths of Irene and Jeremy were forthcoming, John Paget and his sister Debra were in contact with one another.

Each had on different occasions pressed the Coroner's Office for Jeremy's autopsy report, only to be told that the analysis was still underway. But after Schmunk ruled Jeremy's death "undetermined" in August, John and his sister had a talk. For the first time each considered the possibility that maybe, just maybe, their brother-in-law was behind the deaths somehow.

Even considering the possibility of Jack's involvement seemed bizarre. But then, the circumstances of the deaths were bizarre.

Besides, they thought, how well did they really know Jack, anyway?

Debra Paget-Harris' husband Mike was a police officer in New Jersey. Certainly Mike Harris was aware that sometimes people did things their relatives could not bring themselves to believe.

John, Debra, and Mike tossed around the possibility of Jack's involvement, but realized they had nothing to go on—and, after all, if Jack had murdered (there it was, the word was finally out) Irene and Jeremy, he hadn't left a single clue as to how he had done it, at least according to Schmunk.

INTERLUDE WITH WYNONNA

1993–1994

Seventeen

In the aftermath of Jeremy's death, many of Jack's friends and coworkers felt an outrush of pity for Jack Barron. Among these was Patty Bednarczyk, who had after all introduced Jack to Irene only a few years earlier.

In addition to his railroad interest, Jack was a dedicated fan of the country singer Wynonna Judd. Judd's harmonic mixture of country ballad and modern music appealed to Jack. As it happened, Patty Bednarczyk was good friends with the president of the Wynonna Judd fan club. After Jeremy died, Patty had contact with the president of the fan club, who then personally brought Jack's plight to the attention of the singer herself.

Soon Judd was on the telephone to Jack, expressing her condolences at his recent losses. Jack later boasted to Denise Call that Judd had stayed on the telephone with him for more than two hours. During the conversation, Judd arranged for Jack to attend one of her concerts in California, the Feather River Jam. Jack went to the concert, leaving Ashley behind with Roberta.

There Jack posed for a photograph with Judd backstage. Judd gave Jack two more backstage passes for a future show in Reno, and told him to make sure that the next time he brought Ashley with him. Jack did.

Meeting Judd was a major event in Jack's life, it appears. Later, neighbors and friends would remark on how all the photographs of Irene at the Southbreeze house and been taken down, and how they had been replaced by those of Wynonna Judd. At work, Jack boasted that he and Judd were dating, and dropped suggestions that they might get married.

Later, Jack's co-workers and relatives would remark upon Jack's seeming fascination with the country music star. Few believed Jack's assertions that Ms. Judd had a romantic interest in him; to them, it seemed incredible.

But then, some thought, that was Jack: teller of tall tales, always building himself up, trying to make himself look larger than life.

Denise Call recalled the way Jack gushed over Wynonna.

"He went on and on about how beautiful she was," Denise said. "How down-to-earth she was, that she was a real person, not a big star. Or how he got to eat with her, to be with her backstage, and how she was so nice to Ashley. He sent me a copy of the picture that they'd taken with him and her and Ashley."

Denise wasn't sure quite what to make of all this talk from Jack. Why would Jack be going around boasting about his relationship with Judd? When she thought about it, Denise concluded that this was all due to some desperate need in Jack to be the center of everyone's attention.

And upon recollection, Denise remembered nights playing cards with Jack and Irene. Jack took it all so seriously, she remembered.

"When he won, it was, 'I won, I won, you lost!' He'd gloat and gloat and gloat," Denise recalled. "When he lost, he'd get mad." Once when the Barrons and the Calls were playing penny-ante poker, and Jack lost, he threw his cards down, told Irene, "We're going," and they walked out the door.

Eventually Cliff and Denise suspected that Jack wasn't

above cheating at card games. Denise told this to Irene, who said it couldn't possibly be true. Denise told Irene how Jack was doing it, and the next time the couples played cards, they caught Jack. Steadfastly, unemotionally, Jack denied it, although even Irene was convinced that Jack was lying.

To Denise's mind, it was as if Jack couldn't stand being what he really was, that it wasn't good enough. Always there had to be some sort of saga, some drama, in which Jack played the starring role. That was what the Wynonna Judd interlude showed, she thought: Jack's need to be someone, to be seen as powerful, as worthy, as worth the interest of a famous star. He was, she concluded, a little boy trapped in an adult's body, his psychic needs for domination and control at the forefront of his personality, spiraling out of an appalling lack of self-esteem. And when she thought even deeper about it, she could see how Irene had accepted Jack for what he was, how she had made allowances for him.

Irene, Denise thought, always had cared for the weak and the defenseless; and at heart, that's what Jack was, a little boy terrified about what it meant to be a man.

SACRAMENTO

Sunday, August 7, 1994

Eighteen

As 1993 turned into 1994, nothing very much changed in the lives of the surviving Barrons or Roberta Butler. Jack continued to work his regular shift at the Lucky's supermarket, while the senior Pagets or Roberta often took care of little Ashley.

Ashley was a sweetheart. Despite the loss of her mother and her brother, she evidenced all of the gentleness and happy disposition that had so marked her mother. She was, in short, a joyful child.

"She wasn't so standoffish as her brother," John Paget recalled. "She'd come up to you and climb into your lap."

To Roberta's friend Bea Kennedy, who had three daughters of her own and who often took care of Ashley in 1993 and 1994, it was as if the little girl longed for her own family.

"The baby was really comfortable with us," Bea recalled. "She enjoyed playing with my three girls. She frequently called me mommy. She wanted a family so bad, she wanted to fit in. A lot of the time, when it was time to leave, Ashley would cry. She didn't want to go, she wanted to stay here."

At one point, in fact, she and Roberta talked about the

Kennedys adopting Ashley, but Jack refused to consider the notion.

Jack also continued to take Ashley to visit her maternal grandparents. Both Jack and Norma, especially after Jeremy's death, watched her very closely for any sign of illness, as did Bea and Roberta.

Despite the inconclusive results from the attempts to find out what had killed Irene and Jeremy, Jack himself didn't seem that concerned about Ashley's future. As noted, he had failed to follow through on the heart-monitoring test for his daughter. Still, the Pagets and Roberta remained worried. As long as no one could explain what had happened, they figured, Jack had to take precautions.

Accordingly, in early January of 1994, Jack retained a practical nurse, Jill Presley, to work as a baby-sitter for Ashley while he was at work. Jack told her that Ashley had a heart condition, and that she needed to pay particular attention to her breathing.

For most of the spring and into the summer of 1994, Jill kept watch over Ashley. On no occasion did Ashley ever give Jill cause for concern, at least medically speaking.

John Paget, meanwhile, became engaged in a silly feud with his father, Jack Paget, over their own sometimes fractious relationship. What began with words over the telephone was followed up by a letter from Jack telling his son that he didn't need any more heartache in his life. John, as stubborn as his father in his own way, threw up his hands and decided to simply terminate contact with his parents for awhile, and there matters rested for most of the first half of the year.

On August 6, 1994, Roberta brought Ashley back to the house on Southbreeze after a visit with friends in Roseville, a small town just east of Sacramento. Despite a modest cold, Ashley had seemed her normal, energetic self. That night, after Roberta left to return to Benicia and Ashley went to bed, Jill Presley arrived at the Southbreeze house to take charge of Ashley while Jack went to work. It was about 10:45 P.M.

Greeting Jill, Jack told her that Ashley was asleep, and that he had last checked her about half an hour before. Jack gave Jill some iced tea, then left for work.

About midnight, Jill said later, she checked on Ashley. The little girl appeared to be asleep, facing the wall and lying on her right side in the bed. She was wearing "101 Dalmatians" pajamas.

Shortly thereafter, Jill herself fell asleep.

About 4 A.M. Jill woke up and needed to use the bathroom. Next Jill checked again on Ashley. This time she found Ashley lying on her back with the covers off. Jill went into the bedroom and put her hand on Ashley's stomach; it was cold and hard. Jill tried to shake Ashley awake, but she wouldn't come around.

Jill ran out of the room and dialed 911. The emergency operators told Jill to start CPR. She put Ashley on the bedroom floor and tried to open her mouth but couldn't. Jill tried to pry Ashley's mouth open with a washcloth but was unsuccessful.

The EMTs arrived a few minutes later, followed by the Sheriff's patrol deputies. They found Jill in a hysterical state. Ashley was still on the floor. When the EMTs began to treat Ashley, they could find no pulse or signs of breathing. Indeed, lividity had already begun and rigor mortis had set in at the neck, legs and arms.

From the lividity and rigor, EMT Chris Hanson guessed that Ashley had been dead at least four hours.

Nevertheless, the EMTs bundled Ashley off to the hospital, while the deputies called the department's crime scene investigation unit to come to the scene to take photographs.

Meanwhile, Jill herself was in need of medical attention. EMT Ed Crawford recalled that Jill was very upset, blaming herself for Ashley's death. Jill told the EMTs that Jack had warned her never to fall asleep because of Ashley's heart condition. Yet she'd dozed off, exactly as Jack had told her not to do. And now Ashley Ann Barron was dead, just like Irene and Jeremy before her.

Ashley's tiny remains arrived at the Kaiser Hospital about 4:30 A.M. By now, of course, the Barron family tragedy was well-known among the hospital staff.

But if Dr. Schmunk had believed that some mysterious malady was stalking the Barrons, at least one nurse at the Kaiser facility wasn't buying a bit of it.

She called the Sacramento County Coroner's Office to notify it that yet another Barron had died, and minced no words:

"This is murder," Cindy Hayhurst told Coroner's Deputy Billy Guillot.

Guillot was certain that Hayhurst had the situation pegged perfectly. He called the Sheriff's homicide unit to let them know another Barron was dead, and left a message for a detective to call him as soon as possible. Then he pulled the coroner's files on the other Barrons.

Nineteen

Jack was at work while these events unfolded; or at least, that's where the EMTs found him when they told him by telephone of Ashley's death.

Jack left work immediately and drove to the hospital, where he learned that the Coroner's Office would begin another investigation of a death in his family. Then he drove home to spread the bad news.

"Denise, are you sitting down?"

"What?"

"Ashley's gone."

Denise exploded at Jack.

"How can this be?" she shouted. "Jack, three people in the same family can't die for no reason. What are you doing? What's going on?"

Jack mumbled something about some sort of toxic waste in the neighborhood, and said the experts were going to do some tests. He didn't care anymore, Jack said. He was going to move, just give up the house, abandon it. He said he was going to move to Klamath Falls, Oregon, to get away from all the bad memories. Dave was going to help him get a job.

Denise hung up the telephone, furious with Jack. She told Cliff the news. Cliff just shook his head. By now both he and Denise were almost but not quite convinced that Jack had to be a murderer.

The first John Paget heard of any of these events was later the same afternoon.

For most of the year, John had maintained communications silence with Jack and Norma Paget. What information each side received was communicated through third parties, like John's aunts and uncles or his sister and brother.

Thus, when John's secretary told him that his uncle was on the telephone with "bad news," and that he wanted to talk to him, John's immediate concern was that something bad had happened to his parents.

"And so," John recalled later, "I got on the phone, and Les informed me that Ashley was found in her bed in the early morning by her baby-sitter, and that she had died in her sleep."

"You've got to be kidding," John told Les. "This is bizarre. There's just no way she died in her sleep."

"I know, John," Les said. "We don't know anything yet. I do know you and your father have been having problems this past year, but you need to know that they need you right now."

John thought this over.

"This is really going to be tough," he told Les. "I don't know what to do."

"You're just going to have to forget about the past and take care of business," Les told him. "They need you right now."

John let a few hours pass, trying to figure out how he should make the telephone call and what he should say, in light of the estrangement.

"Eventually I picked up the phone, and my mother answered," John recalled.

"I just heard a couple of hours ago about Ashley," John

told Norma. "I just don't know what to say, I'm so sorry. I just want you to know that I'm taking the next plane that I can and I'll be there to be in support of you and the rest of the family."

"Under the circumstances, John, we don't want you here," Norma told her son.

John felt this as a stab in the heart.

"That was the last thing I needed to hear from my mother," he recalled. But John was determined to do what he could to ease his parents' pain. He persisted.

"Well, Mom," he said, "maybe you don't and that's okay, if that's the way you feel. But I'm still going to be there, because maybe someone else needs me. Besides that, Ashley was my niece, I was as fond of her as you were, and I intend to be there. I'm not going to cause any scene, I'm not going to impose myself on you if you don't want me to be around. Can I talk to Dad?"

"I don't know if he'll talk to you," Norma told John. "Just a minute."

A minute or so later Jack Paget picked up the telephone.

"I just told Mom, I'm going to be there for Ashley's funeral," John told his father. "I'm going to be there to support the family in any way I can. I know that you folks are having some difficulties with me, and now with Ashley on top of everything, I know things are really tough for you, and I just want you to know that I'm here if you want me."

"Thanks, John," Jack Paget told his son. "Do what you have to do."

This was hardly a ringing cry of enthusiasm, John thought.

"So I'm thinking, boy, that was pretty bad," John recalled. "You know how they say, things are never as bad as you expect or as good as you hope?"

"This one was as bad as I expected. So I said to myself, 'Well, I can't be in control of their feelings, I can only control my own.'

"I'm going to go ahead and come on up," John told his father.

John flew into Sacramento the following day. He rented a car and got a hotel room, where he met one of his aunts, his father's sister, and her family. The aunt told John that a family dinner was being planned, and that they wanted John to attend.

John shook his head no.

"I can't go out to dinner if Mom and Dad are going to be there," he told his aunt. "They don't want to see me."

"No, Les insisted that you come," John's aunt said.

John gave in, dreading the scene and the freeze-out he was expecting.

"So, okay, I went up to the dinner," he recalled. "And when we got there my mother and father were there with Ruth and Les. And I walked in the room, and they both broke down in tears and came over and hugged me, and all was forgiven. And not a word about that situation has been spoken since."

Here it was, then: the essential, all-too-human difference between the Barrons and the Pagets: the capacity to forgive, and to love.

Twenty

The day before, the tiny remains of Ashley Ann Barron, still wearing her "101 Dalmatians" pajamas, were on the autopsy table of Dr. Gregory Reiber, one of the contract pathologists employed by the Sacramento County Coroner's Office.

By this time, Dr. Schmunk had left the partnership that contracted with the county. According to the Coroner's Office, Schmunk's departure had nothing to do with his earlier failure to find the cause of death of Irene and Jeremy, but was instead related to issues involving workload and compensation. Eventually, Dr. Schmunk became the county medical examiner in Green Bay, Wisconsin.

Reiber was 39 years old, and a veteran of nearly 4,000 autopsies. A graduate of Loma Linda University School of Medicine, Reiber was the son of a pathologist, and as a young student had spent his summers working part-time around the Loma Linda Medical Center. From an early age, then, Reiber had been exposed to the requirements for medical-legal autopsies.

In fact, the entire field fascinated Reiber.

The challenge, as Reiber saw it, was in the puzzle-solving. Rather than working on a part of something, such as the examination of a sample of diseased tissue, the forensic pathologist was given the big picture to work with—the whole body, to say nothing of the conditions that surrounded a death. And rather than being tied down in a hospital, the forensic pathologist had interactions with a host of others, including police officials, lawyers, and judges, all in quest of some sort of determination of truth. For Reiber, it could be exhilarating, especially when a key that might unlock a mystery was discovered.

Now Reiber had the Barron mystery to work on.

Reiber began his autopsy examination of little Ashley about 9 A.M. on the morning she was discovered by Jill Presley. The father of two children himself, it was particularly hard to see such a small child in such a condition. But Reiber knew he had to be professional and put his emotions completely aside if he was going to do Ashley any good.

"You have to separate the part of you that abhors what's been done to a child," he said later, "so you can keep it objective. You want to bring it to court so justice can be done."

Reiber's initial examination of Ashley showed some amount of blood had run from her nose, and an additional amount in her mouth. But he could find no other external evidence of injury, not even the minute eye hemorrhages that Schmunk had found with Irene and Jeremy.

Soon Reiber moved into his internal examination, and this, too, provided no clues. Nowhere did Reiber find evidence of any trauma—no injuries to Ashley's neck muscles, no lung hemorrhages, no brain bruises. In the end, Reiber took samples from all of Ashley's internal organs for further testing, along with Ashley's heart, brain, and spinal cord.

At the conclusion of the autopsy, Reiber was almost as mystified as Schmunk had been with Irene and Jeremy—at least as to the cause of death. As for the manner of death, Reiber had a very strong idea: murder.

"I'm thinking to myself, 'Hey, I've got Barron number three here,'" Reiber recalled later. "And naturally, I'm suspicious as hell, because this doesn't make any sense."

After completing the autopsy, Reiber pulled the case files of Jeremy and Irene in the hope that something might jump out at him. But nothing did, at least right away.

While Reiber was doing this, Coroner's Deputy Billy Guillot was trying to pull together some basic information about the Barron family. Like Nurse Hayhurst, Guillot was convinced in his own mind that the death of Ashley Barron was a case of murder; and like her, he was highly suspicious of Jack. He resolved to find out what had happened, and this time, get the Sheriff's Department something it could use to get after Jack. And as it turned out, Billy was relentless.

Guillot was 33 years old, and a native of the bayou country of northern Louisiana. After graduating from high school, Billy joined the Air Force, and was sent to Minot, North Dakota.

"I was a gas station attendant for KC-135 tankers," he said. "That's all I did, fill 'em up."

After getting out of the Air Force, Billy joined the Monroe County Sheriff's Department, which paid him the grand sum of $800 a month. "It was a little like Barney Fife," he recalled. "We had guns but no bullets." Presumably, Guillot was kidding.

But soon Billy and his wife were the parents of two small children, and the $800 salary just wasn't going to cut it.

"I had some friends here in Sacramento," he said, "with the Probation Department. They suggested that I come on up here and see if I couldn't get on with the Sacramento Sheriff's Department." Billy thought this was a good idea, especially when he found out what the Sheriff was paying his deputies—nearly three times the rate for Monroe County's finest.

Packing up all their belongings in a truck, the Guillots

headed for Sacramento. When they arrived, Billy took the test for Sheriff's deputy, but there were no openings.

Instead, Billy found an opening as an investigator with the Coroner's Office.

His first few days on the job were "pretty morbid," Billy admitted; but there was only one way to get used to the work, and that was "to hold your breath and do it. You've got to see what happened."

But people can get used to anything if they experience it every day, and Billy was no exception. By the time of Ashley Barron's death, Billy had been a coroner's deputy for almost eight years, and there was little that could amaze him anymore.

After reviewing the earlier Barron files, Billy began making and taking telephone calls. One of his first was from Detective Paul Spreitzer, the on-duty homicide detective, who was returning Guillot's earlier call. Billy wanted to find out from Spreitzer what the Sheriff's Department had done so far.

"I was trying to encourage their involvement," he said later.

Spreitzer told Billy that crime scene technicians had been to the Barron house, photographs had been taken, and that a crime scene diagram had been drawn. Beyond that, Spreitzer said, there wasn't much that could be done, pending the autopsy.

According to Spreitzer, it appeared that Jack had left for work around 11 P.M., and that he been at work from midnight on.

That meant, it also appeared, that Jack couldn't have had anything to do with Ashley's death. After all, hadn't Jill Presley seen Ashley at midnight in one position, and in another position four hours later? That meant Ashley had to be alive some time after Jack had begun his workshift, it appeared.

Billy understood this reasoning, but couldn't shake the

feeling that Jack was still responsible, somehow. It was the only way the three deaths made any sense.

Billy pulled the telephone closer and began making more telephone calls. One of his first went to Jack Barron.

At 8:45 A.M. Billy reached Jack at home, and confirmed Jack's departure for work at about 11 P.M. To Billy, Jack seemed reserved, even stoic. So did Roberta, when, half an hour later, she called to find out what was going on.

Neither Jack nor Roberta seemed very emotional about Ashley's death. That wasn't that unusual in Guillot's experience, particularly among middle-class whites who often made it a primary point to maintain their dignity in times of loss. It was only later that Billy began to wonder whether even then, however, Roberta Butler had begun to suspect that her own son may have killed her daughter-in-law and her grandchildren.

Twenty-one

Another service at St. Paul's, another ceremony at St. Mary's. This time Jack didn't buy a plot for Ashley. He ordered her remains cremated and the ashes placed on top of Jeremy's coffin.

The families again gathered at the Southbreeze house. Jack and Norma Paget, John and his sister Debra, Roberta Butler, her sister Jeanne Dillon, and Tim O'Keefe, Roberta's boyfriend. *The same old crowd*, John thought. *This is completely bizarre.*

Shortly afterward, Jack and Dave arrived at the house, carrying an enormous floral arrangement that had been sent to Jack by Wynonna Judd. Jack was wearing a T-shirt that said "Wy's Guy."

John watched Jack and Dave come in with the flowers.

"He came in with his friend Dave," John recalled, "and the two of them were joking back and forth and laughing and having just a wonderful time. And he had just come back from the cemetery after burying his daughter's ashes on top of the graves of the other two!"

Jack and Dave talked a lot about Wynonna—how she'd called Jack once more, how nice she was, and about her flowers for Ashley. Both Jack and Dave seemed really up, and John was sickened by what he saw as Jack and Dave's party-time behavior.

His sister Debra caught his eye and seemed to read his mind.

"And Debra took one look at me and I took one look at her, and she motioned to me to come into the living room where nobody was," John recalled. Brother and sister then had a short conversation.

"Can you believe this?" Debra asked.

"No, I'm absolutely appalled," John told his sister. "What do you want to do?"

"I've just got to get out of here," Debra said. "I don't care where we go, but we ought to get out of here."

"Well, it's going to look funny for us to leave right now," John said.

"I don't care."

John thought about this for a minute.

"You know, you're right, I don't care either," he said. "What do you say we take it down to the Coroner's Office to let them know exactly what we've just witnessed?"

Both John and Debra were convinced in their own minds that Jack had murdered Irene, Jeremy, and now Ashley. The scene at the Southbreeze house and the seeming celebration over the flowers from Wynonna had been the last straw.

That same afternoon John and Debra arrived at the Coroner's Office, where they met Deputy Coroner Bob Bowers. John and Debra described the scene at the house and Jack's behavior, and put it quite bluntly: Jack had to be a murderer, there was no other explanation.

"We told them we came there specifically to report what we had just been through," John recalled, referring to the scene at the Southbreeze house.

"Because we felt it bore on the potential investigation. We all but said—we did say—we think Jack's involved. I think we were also curious as to what they thought, at that point. See, by this time, we'd already been through the previous two, and nothing was being accomplished. No progress was being made. We were kind of saying, 'Now dammit, what more do you need? Get on with program. What are you going to do? Are you looking at this as a homicide?' "

By this time, the news of Ashley's death had spread through every corner of the Coroner's Office, and the broad consensus was that some sort of foul play had to be involved.

"When Ashley died," Bowers recalled, "we knew then in the office—we were saying to each other—we had a set of serial murders on our hands."

And there was only one logical suspect.

But Bowers, while sympathetic to Debra and John, was inclined to be cautious with any pronouncements.

"We didn't want to get the family upset," Guillot recalled, even though it was pretty clear that John and Debra *were* upset. But Bowers assured the Paget siblings that the Coroner's Office was concerned about the situation, and that they weren't about to look the other way.

But in the light of Reiber's preliminary findings on Ashley, there was too little to go on. Reiber had already explained to Guillot and Bowers that if Ashley had been suffocated, it might be impossible to tell from the medical evidence; sometimes, he said, it was impossible to distinguish the characteristics of a suffocation death from one of natural causes, especially with a child as young as Ashley.

John and Debra left the Coroner's Office, still frustrated.

But Debra and John's personal visit was hardly necessary to set the Coroner's Office buzzing with activity. Everyone in the office now began to discuss the cases, suggesting possible approaches. It just seemed impossible that three different people could die, and no one could say what the causes were. A decision was made to pull out all the stops in an effort to eliminate anything, however remote, before coming to the now seemingly inevitable conclusion that the three Barrons had to have been suffocated.

Given Jack's apparent absence from the scene at Ashley's death, and possibly Irene's, discussion turned to possible poisons. Normal toxicological screening did not detect every type of poison; it was more efficient for the experts to suggest a type of poison, then run tests to determine whether the victim's blood showed any traces of the substance.

An order was issued for the production of Jeremy and Irene's blood samples from the earlier autopsies. Each would be subjected to a wide-ranging toxicological screening. But almost immediately, this process ran into problems; it appeared that all the samples from Irene's autopsy had been thrown away.

"Dead end," a coroner's deputy scrawled across the request.

Samples of Jeremy's blood, however, had been retained, and these were tested for fenadryl, an extremely potent synthetic narcotic said to be perhaps 100 times as powerful as heroin. Ashley's blood was subjected to similar tests. Altogether, the testing would take almost two months to complete.

In the meantime, however, a coroner's deputy named Laura Synhurst had been reviewing the three Barron files, and on August 19, 12 days after Ashley's death, she noticed something very odd.

If one assumed that Irene Barron had died the night before her body was discovered, and that Ashley had died after midnight on the day she was discovered, an amazing coincidence arose: each had died on the seventh of the month: Irene on June 7, 1992, Jeremy on January 7, 1993, and Ashley on August 7, 1994. Even more amazing: each day was a Sunday.

Twenty-two

Three days later an extraordinary meeting was convened in Bob Bowers' office. Eight people were present, including Bowers, Reiber, Guillot, criminalist James Beede from the crime lab, and Detective Spreitzer from the Sheriff's Department.

By some accounts, the meeting was fractious.

Bowers began by passing out file copies of the three Barron cases. Bowers pointed out Synhurst's discovery: that all the deaths appeared to have occurred on the seventh of the month, and on a Sunday.

If these had been natural deaths, Bowers pointed out, the odds of something like that happening would have been astronomical.

If the deaths were murders—and given the coincidences of the dates and days, that seemed the only logical explanation—the only real suspect was Jack Barron. And since it now appeared that Jack was intent on selling his house and leaving the area, it was imperative for the authorities to decide what to do before he got away.

Reiber then reviewed each of the cases. From his most recent review of Schmunk's autopsy report, it appeared to him that there *was* in fact evidence of strangulation or suffocation in the case of Irene Barron. Reiber pointed out all the petechial hemorrhages in Irene's eyes, lungs, and brain. These could be the result of Irene's blood vessels bursting as she fought for air, he said. Such hemorrhages were common in asphyxial deaths.

Reiber had to admit, however, that some of this apparent trauma might have been caused by natural physical changes to the body after death. But Reiber said the scene was nevertheless otherwise indicative of foul play—primarily, the pillow found over Irene's face by Christina Hamilton, a pillow with apparent streaks of mascara on it, as had been noted by Schmunk.

Now it was Beede's turn. He told the group that an analysis of the stomach contents retrieved from Ashley's remains showed that Ashley had died shortly after her last meal—roast beef, potatoes, and corn. That was consistent with the notion that perhaps she had been dead even before Jill Presley arrived at the house.

That, of course, was inconsistent with the sevens; had Ashley really died shortly after dinner (a possibility also consistent with the extent of rigor mortis and lividity present when she was discovered), she would have died on the sixth, not the seventh. But in fact, this might have been a clue: maybe it wasn't the date of the death that was significant, but the date of the *discovery* of the victim. Either way, it seemed to suggest to those present that the seventh of the month might have significance to the killer, along with the day of Sunday.

Bowers summarized: it seemed now clear that a serial murder case had been going on under their noses for two years; three people were dead and no one could explain how or why. He wanted Detective Spreitzer to agree to a cooperative investigation between the Coroner's Office and the Sheriff's Department. Most importantly, he wanted Spreitzer's department to agree to more interviews with Jill Presley and Jack Barron.

Put on the spot, Spreitzer agreed that the information so far developed by the Coroner's Office was interesting and provocative. He would, he said, present these findings to the rest of the homicide squad for further discussion. But Spreitzer said that at this stage of the game he doubted that any further interview with Jack would be productive.

Then Spreitzer dropped the capper, as recorded by Guillot's notes of the meeting:

"Det. Spreitzer [Guillot wrote] added that even with a confession of guilt from Jack Barron, the lack of corroborating evidence would discourage the DA's office from attempting to prosecute the case."

So it went, as both sides continued chasing their tails: the Coroner's Office wanting the Sheriff's Department to assist in finding the corroboration, and the Sheriff's Department saying it would be fruitless to look for the corroboration unless the Coroner's Office could corroborate that a murder had actually occurred.

Bowers ended the meeting by telling Spreitzer that his office wasn't about to drop the matter. A request had been made, Bowers said, for the services of a psychological profiler from the California Department of Justice—a clear indication that the Coroner's Office was prepared to go over the heads of the Sheriff's Department if that's what it took to get action.

On that acrimonious note, the meeting ended.

Billy Guillot was intrigued by Synhurst's idea about the sevens. When he reviewed the files, he could find no particular significance in the date; but then Guillot noticed that there was very little information about Jack's father in any of the files.

Moreover, Guillot had learned something else, this time from Debra Harris. While at the Southbreeze house after the funeral, Debra told Guillot, Roberta Butler had mentioned that Ashley had died on the same day that Jack's father, Elmore, had been born. Now Guillot wondered: was this significant?

On August 29, Guillot called the Southbreeze house. No

one answered. He left a message on the recorder, asking Jack to call him at the office.

At 1:15 in the afternoon, Roberta called Guillot. Billy explained that he wanted to collect some background on the health history of the Barron side of the family. Roberta was not very cooperative.

"Roberta Butler confirmed that among other members of her family there had been a case of diabetes and one stroke," Guillot noted for the file, "but none of these involved children. There had been no SIDS deaths in her family. Roberta Butler advised that Elmore Barron, the father of Jack Barron, had a similar background. Roberta Butler believes that Elmore Barron has had more children since their divorce but does not know anything about their medical history."

Then Guillot added the following interesting observation:

"Roberta Butler seemed guarded or defensive over the issue of there being the possibility of a genetic medical problem relating to her side of the family. I had stated that the medical records had researched Irene's family, but never Jack's. Roberta Butler replied that 'there was no need to.' Roberta Butler advised that she would be at Jack Barron's residence for the rest of the week helping him move."

From her efforts to cut short the discussion, Billy got the feeling from Roberta that inquiring about the Barron family medical history was, to Roberta, "completely uncalled for."

About half an hour after this conversation, Jack himself called Guillot. Guillot's most pressing interest at this point was to discover the year of Elmore Barron's birth; that way he could determine the day of the week on which Jack's father had been born. If it was also a Sunday, that would be very significant information, Billy thought. But first he needed the year to determine that.

To Guillot, Jack seemed mostly guarded, as Roberta had seemed angry. Jack's tone was clipped, almost nonresponsive. He dismissed Guillot's questions about the Barron family medical history, and turned once more to the Pagets, relating information about Jack Paget's family as though it might be significant.

This was not what Guillot was interested in, of course. But Jack was so cautious Guillot decided he needed to use all his guile, to play Jack as if he were a particularly old and crafty catfish. Gingerly, Guillot broached the question of Elmore's birth date.

"Jack stuttered," Guillot recalled later. "He said that he couldn't remember. I had to press the question." Still Jack said he could not recall.

At length, however, Jack did recall Elmore's Social Security number, and provided a state where Jack believed that Elmore had resided.

Guillot ran Elmore's name, day and month of birth, state of residence, and Social Security number through a law enforcement computer system. Eventually the right Elmore popped up, along with the year of birth—1938.

Billy checked a perpetual calendar for August 7, 1938. It was a Sunday. Jack's sudden nervousness over his father's birth date, and his obvious reluctance to provide the information told Guillot he was on the right track.

"I'd hit a hot button," Guillot said later.

Twenty-three

Sometime between Ashley's funeral and the end of the month of August, Jack planted another tree. This one was next to the one commemorating Jeremy, which itself was next to the one commemorating Irene. Then he sold the house, quit his job, and made plans to go camping.

Some of Jack's co-workers later recalled that Jack said he planned to go to Oregon to be with his brother. Since Jack had no brother, it seems likely that he was referring to Dave. After all, he had told Denise shortly after Ashley's death that he was going to abandon the Southbreeze house and move to Klamath Falls, which was the largest town north of Shasta. It was Jack's decision to leave Sacramento that galvanized the officials of the Coroner's Office and led to the unsatisfactory meeting in Bowers' office.

Jack's decision to leave Sacramento had other consequences, as well. Roberta helped Jack prepare for the move by boxing up a number of things that had belonged to Irene. She called the Pagets, by now living in the town of Pilot Hill some 30 miles northeast of Sacramento, and Jack and Norma came in a pickup truck to pick the boxes up. Among the items was a wooden cradle Jack Paget had made for Ashley. The Pagets took the boxes home, and stored them in a pumphouse; for both grandparents, the contents of the boxes were too painful to immediately sort through.

Meanwhile, John Paget and Debra Harris continued to press the Coroner's Office for some sort of action against their former brother-in-law.

As noted, by this time both Debra and John were convinced that Jack had wiped out his entire family. Beneath the pain from the deaths of Irene, Jeremy, and Ashley came the question of why.

Why would Jack do such a thing? There seemed to be no answer other than some sort of madness.

Both John and Debra continued to press the Coroner's Office throughout the fall of 1994. Officials there assured John that they were keeping close tabs on Jack's whereabouts—that they were "tailing" him—although this seems not to have been the case.

Jack had sold the house on Southbreeze Drive, collected another $13,068.61 in death benefits from Ashley's life insurance, had loaded his van, and had then dropped from sight.

No one seemed to know where Jack had gone. And when Billy Guillot brought up the matter of Jack Barron with Sheriff's Detective Rick Lauther one afternoon at the law enforcement firing range in Sacramento, long-dormant bad feelings immediately erupted. Lauther insisted that Jack Barron was innocent of any murder, while Billy maintained the opposite. Some thought that both investigators might come to blows, or even worse, given that both were armed.

Guillot suspected that Lauther believed he was on some sort of wild-goose chase, doubtless precipitated by Guillot's desire to prove he was every bit as qualified as Lauther; while Guillot believed that Lauther had been too long in the job, and was suffering from terminal burnout, and therefore couldn't see the obvious. In the end, cooler heads took control, but relations between the Sheriff's Department and the Coroner's Office took another turn for the worse.

By November, the profiler from the California Department of Justice, Mike Prodan, was part way into his analysis of the Barron deaths; more important, the toxicity studies on Ashley and Jeremy's blood samples had been returned.

Despite tests for a great number of poisonous substances, including fenadryl, all had come back negative. So had bacteriological culture tests of Ashley's blood. As with Irene and Jeremy before her, an intensive examination of Ashley's brain and nervous system showed absolutely no abnormalities.

And at this point, the Coroner's Office, at least, was left with the only possible choice: if all the possibilities but the impossible have been eliminated, it is the impossible that must be the truth. Hoping to get some additional support for the cause, Bowers had sent a complete package of information on the Barron deaths to the Sacramento County District Attorney's Office, where it was routed to Deputy District Attorney Robin Shakely.

Shakely read the file and agreed that, taken together, all of the circumstances of the three Barron deaths were remarkably suspicious.

"She was sort of stirring the pot," as Guillot put it later.

Still, the Sacramento Sheriff's Department refused to open a case in the absence of a definitive medical finding that murder had been committed.

On November 6, 1994, Guillot took a call from Roberta Butler. Roberta wanted to know if the experts had finally been able to determine the cause of Ashley's death. Billy told Roberta that the determination of the cause was still under investigation. Roberta then told Billy that Jack had moved in with her, at her condominium, in Benicia, California. The answer to Jack's whereabouts was now resolved: he'd gone home to Mother.

Two weeks after this, Dr. Reiber finally wrapped up his report on the autopsy of Ashley Barron.

"Cause of death: undetermined," Reiber wrote. He added, "Homicidal violence cannot be excluded."

Irene Paget at 18, selected as Miss Fallbrook, 1974. Irene wanted more than anything to be a wife and a mother. (*Photo by Olan Mills*)

After a false start in a first marriage, Irene moved to Sacramento in 1986, when this photograph was taken. Soon after coming to Sacramento, Irene met Jack Barron. (*Photo by Olan Mills*)

Jack, Irene, Jeremy and Ashley, in the spring of 1992, shortly before Irene's sudden death. To all outward appearances, the Barrons were a typical young family. (*Photo by Olan Mills*)

The Barrons at Easter, 1992. Roberta Butler, Jack Barron's mother, is on the left holding granddaughter Ashley. Two months after this photo was taken, Irene was dead; less than a year later, so was Jeremy. Within three years, all were dead except Jack Barron. (*Photographer unknown, photo courtesy of the Paget family*)

Jeremy Barron at 22 months. After Irene died, Jeremy cried for his mother. Jack Barron told Jeremy that if he didn't stop crying, he'd make sure Jeremy went to where his mother was. Two months later, Jeremy was dead. (*Photo by Olan Mills*)

Ashley Barron, then 4, in a snapshot taken by a family friend on August 6, 1994. The day after this picture was taken, Ashley was found dead in her bed.

(Photo by Tim O'Keefe, courtesy of Bea Kennedy)

Jack, Ashley and country singer Wynonna Judd at Lake Tahoe early in 1994. After hearing about the Barron family's misfortunes, Judd called and corresponded with Jack. Jack told friends that he and Judd might get married. (*Photographer unknown, photo courtesy of the Paget family*)

The Paget family on a recent Mother's Day. Beginning at the third from the left: Paul Paget, Norma Paget, Jack Paget and John Paget. Third from the right are Debra Harris and her husband Mike. John Paget and the Harrises pressed Sacramento County officials to investigate the Barron deaths despite official indifference. (*Photographer unknown, photo courtesy of the Paget family*)

Benicia, California police officers Monty Castillo and Tom Dalby. Dalby, a patrol officer in February, 1995, was the first to question Jack Barron in the death of his mother, Roberta Butler. Castillo investigated the case, eventually turning his information over to Sacramento County authorities for prosecution. Two years later, Dalby (bearded) and Castillo switched jobs, making Castillo the patrol officer and Dalby the detective. Benicia Police believe that periodic job rotation makes police officers sharper. (*Photos by Carlton Smith*)

Coroner's Deputy Billy Guillot and Dr. Gregory Reiber of the Sacramento County Coroner's Office in the autopsy suite. Guillot was convinced the Barrons had been murdered by Jack Barron, but received no assistance from the Sacramento County Sheriff's Department until after the death of Roberta Butler. After Roberta's death, Dr. Reiber reviewed the autopsy of Irene Barron and found evidence of murder. (*Photo by Dr. Robert Anthony, courtesy of Sacramento County Coroner*)

Jack Barron, under arrest by Sacramento County Sheriff's detectives Maryl Lee Cranford, left, and Ted Verdouris, on July 18, 1995. In the background is Monty Castillo. Ironically, Jack's arrest came on what would have been Irene Barron's 37th birthday. (*Photo by Sarah Rohr, copyright* Benicia Herald, *used by permission*)

Roberta Butler. Roberta was feuding with her son Jack in the weeks before she was found dead in her bed February 27, 1995. It was Roberta's death, ruled a homicide, that led eventually to Jack's arrest on charges that he murdered his entire family.

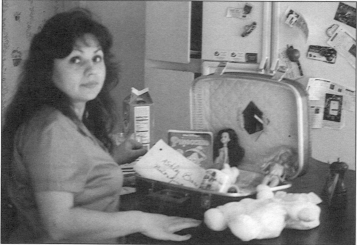

Bea Kennedy, Roberta's closest friend in Benicia, with Ashley's traveling suitcase containing her dolls, crayons and *Pinocchio* book. Ashley often stayed with Bea and her family. After Ashley's death, Roberta gave Ashley's suitcase to Bea to remember her by. (*Photo by Carlton Smith*)

Twenty-four

In retrospect, Reiber's autopsy report on Ashley Barron only focused the most difficult questions about the Barron case.

For, if Reiber could assert that in his judgement, homicidal violence could not be excluded as a cause of Ashley's death—and given that he'd already told the Sacramento Sheriff's Department in late August that he believed Irene had been murdered too—why did he not, at that point, then reopen Irene's file and come to the same conclusion?

After all, now that Reiber had concluded that it was possible that little Ashley had been murdered, what was to prevent him from saying the same, officially, about Irene? And what effect would that have had on the by-now notoriously reluctant Sheriff's Department to commence its own investigation?

More to the point, the medical evidence about Irene's death was far more significant than that of Ashley. In examining Ashley's remains after her death, Reiber found not one single petechial hemorrhage, not one single burst blood vessel in the lungs or brain, or a single bruise in the throat. To every inspection and test, little Ashley's body was as perfect as the day she had been born.

In contrast, Irene had multiple hemorrhaging, along with very suggestive bruising—far more evidence of murder than in the case of Ashley.

So why did Reiber conclude that "homicidal violence cannot be excluded" in Ashley's case, and tell the Sheriff's Department that it looked to him that murder had been committed in Irene's case, yet do nothing more?

Why didn't he argue that Irene's case should be reopened, that a new look should be undertaken of the far more powerful evidence of murder involving Irene?

Years later, that question was propounded to Reiber; and it is a measure of Dr. Reiber's honesty that he confronted the issue directly.

"This is part science, part art," Reiber said of the business of forensic pathology. "It's really a matter of interpretation." When he examined the remains of Ashley Barron and found the possibility of murder, Reiber said, he was the beneficiary of a number of facts not known to Schmunk: about the Sundays, and the sevens, and the reality that two other Barrons had already died. It was Reiber's gut instinct that the situation was ripe for further investigation.

But as for Schmunk's earlier assessment of Irene's death, Reiber in the fall of 1994 felt no compulsion to intensively reexamine his former colleague's findings, even if he indicated his disagreement with them in the meeting of August 22, 1994. In the absence of definitive medical data—demonstrable facts like wounds or crushed larynxes or detected poisons—one had to conclude that Schmunk had done his best and had made his own interpretation, Reiber said later.

What's lost here, of course, is the concept of urgency. If Ashley was dead from homicidal violence, and if a pathologist argued for an interpretation asserting that her mother, Irene, was similarly dead of homicidal violence, the chances seem pretty strong that Jeremy might be dead of homicidal violence. All of this ought to have forced, but did not, some anxiety on the part of the Sacramento Sheriff's Department that, if three were now dead, who was soon to follow?

ARCADIA, CALIFORNIA

Christmas, 1994

Twenty-five

Throughout the fall of 1994, John Paget and his sister Debra Harris discussed whether they should confide their suspicions about Jack to their parents, Jack and Norma Paget.

"Debra and I specifically discussed," John recalled, "what should we tell Mom and Dad. And because we didn't have any proof, and we hadn't received anything from the authorities to give us any indication that this was the direction things were heading, we thought it was premature. We were afraid to start pointing fingers too publicly and to cause my parents undue [stress], if that's what it turned out to be."

But the subject of murder couldn't be contained forever.

"At Christmastime, we were in Arcadia at my father's sister's home," John recalled. "And my mother asked me a question, point-blank."

"John," Norma told her son, "I've been talking to some people, and everyone we talk to always asks the question— if it's possible that Jack had anything to do with this."

John realized he was going to have to tell his parents what he and Debra had been thinking and discussing, and what they had been doing in relaying information to the Coroner's Office.

"Well, I have some thoughts on that subject," John told Norma. "Let's get Dad in here. I need to talk to you."

John felt unsure how Jack and Norma were going to take the news that the deaths might have been caused by their son-in-law.

"But the way she asked the question," John recalled, "gave me some confidence that they were going to accept the possibility okay. Of course, my sister Debra wasn't there to share in this with me. She's in New Jersey, and I'm thinking, well, I'm just going to have to do this on my own, and I think that it's time they find out."

Jack Paget came into the room, along with his sister, John's aunt, who knew what John and Debra had been thinking.

"Debbie and I have for some time felt that Jack is responsible for these deaths," John told his parents. "We think that he killed all three of them."

To John's surprise, neither his mother nor his father was shocked at this suggestion. Instead they wanted to know how long John had been thinking this way.

"Since Ashley, anyway," John said. "Since Ashley's death. We weren't certain before Ashley, we had toyed with the thought about it, but we didn't want to bring our suspicions to you, because we didn't want to cause you any undue upset."

"Well, other people have been telling us this," Norma said, "and we just didn't—"

Jack Paget broke in.

"People have talked to us about this," he said, "but I just didn't think Jack was smart enough. I never thought Jack was smart enough to commit murder and cover it up so the authorities couldn't detect it."

John led his mother and father through the reasoning that led to the consideration that Jack might be a murderer: the lack of any medical evidence to show how the three Barrons had died, Jack's new "roommate" so soon after Irene's death, his unemotional behavior at the funerals of

Jeremy and Ashley, the convenience of the double plot, the coincidence of Ashley's death on Jack's father's birthday, the seeming fascination with Wynonna Judd.

"Remember how Jack acted at each one of the funerals?" John asked, but Jack Paget seemed to shrug this off.

"Everybody handles death differently," Jack Paget observed. "I just thought with his Catholic upbringing and his involvement with the Church, that he just looked at death as the best thing that can happen to you, you know, you're going on to better and bigger things."

"Well, that's true," John said, "everybody does handle death a little bit differently. But I found it totally bizarre that there was almost this party atmosphere every time one of these circumstances occurred and the family would gather together, and everybody had their arms around Jack and gave him all this attention."

When all the Pagets discussed this further, they agreed that, no matter what had happened, Jack Barron had always been the center of everyone's attention.

That, some later thought, might in fact have been one of the main motives in the deaths of all three Barrons: that Jack was a glutton for sympathy.

Although as a phenomenon, it hasn't received nearly the attention of such child death mysteries as SIDS, it is a demonstrable fact that a significant portion of child deaths and injuries are caused by parents who seek attention for themselves through the ailments of their children.

This is known as Munchausen Syndrome by Proxy—after Baron Karl Friederich Hieronymus Freihess von Munchausen, an eighteenth century German nobleman and war hero, who gained an unwanted notoriety when a writer, one Rudolph Raste, wrote a number of outrageous lies about Munchausen's exploits, and then had the diabolical idea of putting them in Munchausen's own mouth, making them seem as though Munchausen himself was claiming the ludicrously incredible exploits.

Because the tales were so outrageous and patently unbelievable, poor Baron Munchausen was soon believed to be a pathological prevaricator, and his name became virtually synonymous with inveterate, compulsive lying.

Drawing on this theme, in 1951 a physician named Richard Asher invented the term "Munchausen Syndrome" to describe patients who made up stories about nonexistent illnesses and who subjected themselves to unneeded and often painful medical procedures, primarily as a means of getting attention from others, usually doctors.

Twenty-five years later, an English pediatrician, a man named Meadow, extended Asher's concept by coining the term, "Munchausen Syndrome by Proxy," when he investigated the cases of a number of epileptic patients whose mothers had fabricated their children's symptoms.

Munchausen Syndrome by Proxy is not a form of insanity; in other words, the person knows that what they are doing is wrong, and is capable of recognizing the harmful nature of their acts, and is able to take steps to evade detection.

Rather, it is a character disorder—something akin to antisocial behavior, and rooted in excessive narcissism, or overweening love of self.

When in the grip of this syndrome, a person assumes the role of the patient indirectly, and either fakes or causes injuries to another person, usually a child, in order to gain attention for themselves.

While most often appearing in the form of imaginary ills, it is not unknown for parents afflicted with Munchausen Syndrome by Proxy to provide their children with real illness by inducing seizures, bleeding, poisoning, and even suffocation.

While the number of Munchausen Syndrome by Proxy cases has never been quantified, most experts believe they are more common than previously believed, and that they are underreported because of their hidden, criminal origins.

Most of the known cases of Munchausen Syndrome by

Proxy that have been reported in the United States have involved mothers with children under the age of six; one notorious case in New York State resulted in a mother eventually being accused and convicted of the pillow suffocation murders of all of her children, one after another, shortly after birth, over a period of years, all for the sympathy and attention she received from friends and relatives after each death.

But despite the predominance of such cases among women, they are not unknown among men. According to Dr. Marc Feldman, vice-chair of the Department of Psychiatry at the University of Alabama at Birmingham and a nationally recognized expert on Munchausen Syndrome by Proxy, the character disorder has also been known among men.

Feldman estimated that perhaps has many as 15 or 20 cases of Munchausen by Proxy cases involving men as the perpetrators have been documented in medical literature, including one rather famous Israeli case in which the perpetrator first put sedatives in his wife's coffee, then injected her with gasoline while she was passed out. The wife died, and the perpetrator was left with two young children to care for. A nanny was hired to assist, and the man eventually proposed marriage to the nanny, only to be rejected.

The man then put sedatives in the nanny's coffee and injected her with gasoline; this woman survived, although she was rendered a paraplegic. Once convicted, the man fell in love with his male prison cellmate, and having been rejected by him, injected him with turpentine, resulting in his death. Throughout all these deaths, the perpetrator played the role as the loving, put-upon caregiver, even though he was secretly the cause of all the deaths and illness.

Other cases involving men are known to the Federal Bureau of Investigation as well, according to Feldman, including one case in which a man was secretly videotaped by a hidden hospital camera trying to smother his child by forcing her face into the mattress.

"These are people who almost invariably have severe personality disorders," Feldman observed, "longterm, dysfunctional ways of dealing with life in general and stress in particular; they are usually needy, impulsive, and exercise poor judgement."

In most cases of Munchausen by Proxy, Feldman said, one of the primary motives is to build the self-esteem of the perpetrator.

"In some ways it's an exaggeration of the maternal role," he observed. "By making a child somewhat ill, they can then become the exaggerated, indefatigable, beleaguered caregiver."

Taking on that role brings the perpetrator all the attention they seek for themselves, and shifts attention away from their precipitating actions. In situations where the precipitating action proves fatal, Feldman noted, in some cases the perpetrator gets his or her reward at the funeral.

"These people are funeral junkies," he said.

Well, did this apply to Jack Barron? If he had killed, first his wife Irene, then his children, Jeremy and Ashley, was it because he was at his best when everyone else felt sorry for him?

Even as the Pagets were considering what might have driven Jack to murder his own family, another psychological expert was pondering the same question, and coming up with a different answer.

Mike Prodan of the California Department of Justice, a psychological profiler trained by the FBI, had accepted Supervising Coroner Bowers' request for an evaluation of the Barron case.

Prodan was in his mid-forties, after having spent over 20 years as a street cop and special agent for the California Department of Justice. In the mid-1980s he was one of 34 state and local law enforcement officers nationwide to be given special training by the FBI in the art of psychological profiling. Beginning in the late eighties, Prodan had handled about 100 cases a year, many involving serial offenders and, often, horrific homicides.

But for almost all of those cases, one important thing was already known: that murder had definitely been committed. In the case of the Barrons, Prodan didn't even have that. Instead, it was almost the reverse of the usual situation. Where in most cases, Prodan had a known crime to work with and was seeking a possible suspect, in the Barron case, it was the possible suspect who was known and the crime that needed to be determined.

To that end, Prodan's first task was to do what the Sheriff's Department and the Coroner's Office hadn't yet been able to accomplish: determine the likelihood that murder had taken place.

This was called an "equivocal death analysis," in which Prodan was required to weigh all the factors with an eye toward deciding which was most likely: natural death, suicide, or homicide. An important part of making that determination would have to be provided by Jack himself, as the most logical suspect. In other words, if Prodan could determine a reasonable motive for Jack to have committed multiple murder, then he could begin to sort out the possibilities between illness, suicide and homicide.

At least in the initial stages, Prodan considered Munchausen Syndrome by Proxy as a possibility, but soon discounted it.

For one thing, the official American Psychiatric Association diagnostic criteria for Munchausen Syndrome by Proxy specified that there should be no "external incentives," such as financial gain, for the perpetrator. In Jack's case, there were such possible incentives: the life insurance on Irene, Jeremy, and Ashley. Altogether, by the fall of 1994, Jack had collected nearly $41,000 in benefits from the deaths of his wife and children.

Moreover, the pattern of the Barron deaths did not fit the

typical Munchausen profile; in other words, there was no history of long-running health issues involving each of the victims, histories in which Jack would have cast himself as the heroic and long-suffering caregiver. Indeed, the Barrons were reasonably healthy one day and dead the next.

Prodan was much more intrigued about the sevens and the Sundays. Drawing upon information provided by Guillot, gleaned by conversations with Debra Harris and others, Prodan began constructing a psychological assessment of Jack. The key, Prodan believed, was Jack's unsatisfying relationship with his father, Elmore. There was something there, Prodan's instincts told him, that may have led Jack to kill his own family.

SACRAMENTO, CALIFORNIA
January, 1995

Twenty-six

Whether it was because of Reiber's conclusion that homicide could not be excluded as the cause of Ashley's death, or because of Prodan's interest in the case, or Deputy District Attorney Shakely's pot-stirring, or for some other reason, by early December of 1994 the wheels of the Sacramento Sheriff's Department finally began to turn in the Barron matter.

Shakely had given the Barron files to her boss, John O'Mara, the District Attorney's top homicide prosecutor, and asked what he thought.

"She asked me what I think and I said it looks like he's killing these people," O'Mara later told the *Sacramento Bee*.

O'Mara called the Sheriff's Department homicide unit, and asked the supervisor there, Lt. Gabriele Bender, to assign two investigators to the case. But the two investigators O'Mara requested were unavailable.

Meanwhile, as a result of a reorganization in the Sheriff's Department, the investigation of suspected child homicide cases involving family members was transferred from the homicide unit to the child abuse unit. As a result, and likely due to Shakely and O'Mara's prodding, the three files involving Irene, Jeremy, and Ashley, which primarily consisted of the autopsy reports, the initial police "casualty" reports, the photographs taken of Irene on the bed, and the scene diagram from Ashley's death, were routed to child abuse unit supervisor Lt. Lena Maddux.

Maddux looked over the files, which were, after all, pretty skimpy. In early January she called in one of her investigators, Maryl Lee Cranford, and gave her the three files.

"I have this case from homicide," Maddux told Cranford. "There are three deaths, all a year apart. There's no cause of death. The Coroner's Office couldn't say they were homicides, just that it looks suspicious. See what you can do with this."

Cranford was 42 years old and a veteran detective. She had joined the Sacramento Sheriff's Department in the early 1970s as the result of a dare.

Like the Pagets, Cranford had grown up as the child of an Air Force serviceman, who had been stationed at McClellan Air Force Base near Sacramento. In one of the many coincidences that kept cropping up in the Barron case, it's quite likely that Cranford's father at one time might have crossed paths in the Air Force with Jack Paget; both were stationed during the same years at McChord Air Force Base in Tacoma, Washington.

After graduating from high school in Sacramento in 1970, Cranford had gone to work as a restaurant hostess, then a clerk in a flooring company. In early 1972 she obtained a job as a clerk-typist for the California Highway Patrol. It was Cranford's job to key in stolen vehicle reports. She had no real interest in law enforcement at the time; it was just another job.

"I was a hippie girl," she recalled.

At the end of 1972, the Sacramento Sheriff's Department advertised for female deputy applicants. Today, it's difficult to recall the days when women in law enforcement were regarded as something of a bold experiment, but that's how things were in the early 1970s. Two of Cranford's co-workers at the Highway Patrol saw the advertisement and decided to apply. The 20-year-old Cranford said she would too.

When Cranford's friends laughed at her—because of her hippie girl image—"They couldn't see me as a cop," Cranford said—Cranford made up her mind to not only take the tests, but to best her co-workers in the competition.

All three women took the written test. Cranford passed, and one of the two co-workers flunked.

"Right after the written test we were escorted to the gymnasium for the physical test," Cranford said. There were ten stations, including pull-up bars, an obstacle course, and the like. Cranford ran through the physical test with ease, leaving her remaining co-worker gasping in her wake.

"I was in very good physical condition," Cranford said. What the co-workers didn't know about the hippie girl was that she'd been a competitive swimmer for 13 years, and probably could have beaten most men around the course.

Afterward, when Cranford was assigned a date for the oral examination, she began to realize what she'd gotten herself into.

"I thought, no way, I don't want to be a cop," she recalled. But then, she thought, she'd come this far, she might as well take the oral exam.

Cranford passed that test as well, and was told to report to the training academy in February of 1973. At the beginning of the training, Cranford still had her doubts about being a police officer, but after 240 hours of training, the doubts were dispelled—especially since, of all those who had entered the training, only 20, including Cranford, were graduated.

It was only at that point that someone in the Sheriff's Department realized that Maryl was only 20 years old—a year short of the requirement to obtain a police certificate. As a result, Cranford had to work the front desk at the

Sheriff's Department until August, when she finally turned 21.

But the department had special plans for Cranford.

"I could pass for 15 at the time," she recalled, and she still had her hippie girl look. The department's vice unit recruited Cranford to work undercover.

The main target at the time was massage parlors, which had just come into vogue as a prostitution venue. The hippie girl Cranford would go into massage parlors looking for work as a masseuse. The operator of the massage parlor would tell Cranford how the operation worked; meanwhile, another, male, vice officer, would pose as a customer, and reach an agreement with one of the real prostitutes. That way, the vice unit had evidence against both the prostitute as well as the promoter of prostitution.

Altogether, Cranford worked four years as an undercover officer, handling prostitution, drugs, gambling, and other vice and organized crime cases. In the late seventies and early eighties, Cranford worked as a special investigator for the Sacramento District Attorney's Office, in courthouse and airport security, and as a corrections officer in the jail. It was not until the late 1980s that Cranford worked as a regular, uniformed patrol officer; that lasted three years, until she injured her knee jumping over a fence trying to catch a fleeing burglar.

After the knee injury, Cranford took the test for detective, and passed. Her first assignment was in sex crimes and elder abuse—"granny bashing," as the cops called it. In July of 1992, one month after Irene Barron's death, Cranford was assigned to the department's child abuse unit.

The child abuse unit dealt primarily with crimes against children—often, crimes committed by their parents or other caregivers, generally involving neglect or abuse.

Shortly after joining the unit, Cranford was assigned three cases in a row in which a child had died from parental abuse or neglect.

"The first one was horrendous," she recalled. "The

child's life prior to her death was horrifying.''

The conditions of the child's life before her sad end appalled Cranford, who by then had her own children. Cranford took the case personally, which she later came to see as a mistake.

"When you have an innocent little child who can't protect herself, that's when it gets to you," she said. "[But] you have to be a professional. You can't cry, you can't do that. I was never able to grieve that first one, and then came the other two right after. I kind of shut down. I started having problems. I went to a psychologist for two months, then things started getting better. It still hurt, but I managed to control it.''

Still, in her 20-year career as a cop, Cranford found the child abuse investigation unit by far the most satisfying. She recalled a case in which she took an eight-year-old girl into protective custody because of neglect by the mother.

"All she had eaten for months was noodles. She was so malnourished her hair had died," Cranford remembered. "It was dead and broken.''

As Cranford put the child in the back seat of her car and started to drive away, she heard the child say, "Thank you.'' Cranford stopped the car and looked at the eight-year-old in the back seat.

"What?" Cranford asked.

"Thank you," the little girl said again.

"Then she sighed," Cranford recalled. "She said, 'I needed to be away.' ''

Cranford took the Barron files and read them. This was, she understood, to be extra work over and above her normal caseload.

"I read the whole case," Cranford said. "I thought to myself, this is bizarre. There are three victims, and all of them die on Sunday, the seventh of the month? I really felt it was a homicide, but without the [Coroner's Office] reporting a manner of death, we couldn't say for sure *what* it was.''

Cranford next consulted with Guillot and Reiber. She wondered whether some sort of delayed-action poisoning might be involved.

''I started exploring the possibility of arsenic, because they don't test for arsenic,'' she said. ''But they [the Coroner's Office] didn't think arsenic could be involved, because there was no burning of the stomach lining.''

Cranford talked to Rick Lauther and Bob Reisdorph, the detectives who had originally handled Irene's case.

Lauther continued to believe that Irene's death was from some sort of natural cause.

''He felt Jack was sincerely and appropriately upset,'' Cranford said. ''He was crying. Rick really felt he didn't do it.''

At that point, Cranford didn't know what to think. She made a list of things to check about Jack. At the top of her list was a planned telephone call to Roberta Butler.

BENICIA, CALIFORNIA

Winter, 1994–1995

Twenty-seven

The city of Benicia is one of the best-kept secrets in California. A small town of about 20,000 people on the north side of the Carquinez Strait, about 40 minutes northeast of Oakland, it was and remains one of California's most historic cities.

Named for the wife of the Mariano Vallejo, the last Spanish commandante in Alta California, and later one of the Bear Flag revolutionaries who helped overthrow the Mexican government in 1846, General Vallejo formed a real estate partnership with the American consul, Thomas O. Larkin and a third man, Robert Semple, to found the new town on a wide bench that ran down beneath a line of rolling hills to a point dipping into the strait.

With the coming of the Gold Rush, Benicia soon developed into an important intermediate stop on the way to the goldfields. By 1849, the U.S. Army had sited an important installation, the Benicia Barracks, just to the east of the town. A few years later, the Barracks was renamed the Benicia Arsenal, and the facility became the repository for much of the Army's supplies of shot and powder in the Far West. In the same year, a large, two-story brick building in downtown Benicia was donated to the state, and the building became, for more than a year, the state capitol building.

Today it stands as a state historical monument, replete with the desks used by legislators, their newspapers, and their hats, just as if they'd recently adjourned to their after-hours haunt at the Solano Hotel, at First and E Streets, seven years before the Civil War.

Much of old Benicia, including the old Arsenal, is likewise dotted with similar historic structures, including a guardhouse completed in 1852, where a then-obscure U.S. Army lieutenant named Ulysses S. Grant was once tried for a violation of a minor Army regulation. Others who passed through old Benicia in its earliest days included Bret Harte, Mark Twain, Johann Sutter, William T. Sherman, and an uncounted number of governors, senators, clergymen and educators. In early 1861, the first Pony Express pouch was delivered to Benicia en route from St. Joseph, Missouri to San Francisco.

Altogether, there are more than 40 historic sites scattered around the town, most dating from the mid-nineteenth century; as a result, not unexpectedly, old Benicia in recent years has developed as a center for tourism, buttressed by restaurants, art galleries, and antique shops, along with two marinas.

Until the 1960s, Benicia's economy was largely tied to the Arsenal and the military activities there; but in 1964, the Arsenal was closed, and an attempt was made to transform the old military grounds into an industrial park. That effort, coupled with a demand for Bay Area housing in the 1970s and 1980s, resulted in development of the hills north of the old town. By the eighties, Benicia's population had doubled, with most of the new arrivals finding homes in the Southampton development separated from the older part of town by a new freeway.

Even with the growth, Benicia retained the small-town quality that made most of its residents feel secure, the sort of place where most people knew their neighbors, and where the most pressing issue might be the action of the planning commission approving a new convenience store.

Altogether, it was not the sort of place one might expect to find a possible serial killer.

By January, as the rains began to come down in earnest, Jack had been living at his mother's condo for about two months. It wasn't long before frictions began to develop between Jack, Roberta's boyfriend, Tim O'Keefe, and Roberta.

Jack's relationship with Tim had always been difficult. Some who knew Roberta and Tim thought it was because Roberta consistently made Jack the center of her life; while that might have worked when Jack was living with his own family in Sacramento, it was quite a different matter when Jack was directly underfoot.

Tim naturally felt deposed as the object of Roberta's affections; and Jack's personality—his fits of temper and sarcasm, his demands on Roberta—grated on Tim. Eventually the situation escalated into a dispute between Tim and Roberta, and as a result, Tim moved out.

Meanwhile, Jack had to decide what to do with the rest of his life, now that he was no longer working. Now that he no longer had a family to support, it seemed a good time to change directions.

Jack learned about an opening with Amtrak as an assistant conductor. This seemed to be ideal—if he could get this job, he could at last find work he would really enjoy doing. Roberta, as devout as ever, prayed every night with her Rosary, imploring God that Jack should be hired, and that something good could finally come into her only son's life.

As for the deaths of Irene, Jeremy, and Ashley, Roberta was outwardly quick to bristle if anyone suggested that Jack had done anything untoward. Once, Dave Bednarczyk recalled, when he asked Roberta whether she suspected Jack of having anything to do with the deaths, Roberta turned on him.

"She cursed at me," Bednarczyk told the *Sacramento*

Bee newspaper. "She said, 'You're supposed to be his friend.' "

Co-workers at the Safeway store on Military Road in Benicia, where Roberta worked as a produce clerk, soon learned not to make any suggestion that the deaths of Jack's family were anything other than an inexplicable tragedy.

"She was in denial," one of Roberta's co-workers recalled later. "She couldn't believe that her precious son would ever have done anything like that. Especially since Roberta lived for Jack."

In the Safeway employees' monthly newsletter, Roberta wrote about the deaths.

"Most of you know," she wrote, "about my personal losses in the last five years; of course, the worst were losing my two grandchildren. It was the fondest dream to give them the time and opportunities I couldn't give my son as he was growing up. That won't happen now, but from it all I have learned how much people care."

But privately, inside it may have been a different story.

Later, Bea Kennedy, who was perhaps Roberta's best friend in Benicia, believed that Roberta had doubts about her son as early as the death of Jeremy.

"After Irene, she was in shock," Bea recalled. "She kept saying it was genetic. But after Jeremy, she was disturbed, and while she still kept saying it had to be genetic, it was more like she was giving him the benefit of the doubt.

"We had one conversation, where she said, 'I don't know what's going on, but this is not right, first Irene, and now Jeremy.' "

But after Ashley's death, Roberta grew even more disturbed. Beset with inner turmoil, as Bea recalled it, Roberta struggled with tormenting suspicions about Jack.

"In her inner feelings, she doubted this, that this could be true," Bea recalled, "that [it] could actually have happened." But in Roberta's mind, the nagging suspicions continued to grow.

Then on January 25, 1995, the death certificate on Ashley was finally filed, listing Reiber's findings: "Undetermined; homicidal violence cannot be excluded."

Now Roberta had seen something to validate her worst fears.

From that point on, Bea Kennedy came to believe, Roberta was burdened by the worst emotional conflict a mother can endure: the instinctive knowledge that her only son might be a monster who had killed his own children, her only grandchildren.

Twenty-eight

One of those in agreement with Bea about Roberta's inner conflict was Billy Guillot, the Coroner's Office deputy back in Sacramento, although at that point he had never heard of Bea Kennedy, and had had only limited contact with Roberta. But Guillot remembered Roberta's anger and defensiveness during his conversations with her, and he knew that she had learned the results of Reiber's autopsy.

"I think Roberta knew," he said later. "I think she knew right after Ashley. She just didn't want to admit it to anyone, maybe even to herself."

Whether because of Reiber's findings on Ashley or for some other reason, as January turned into February, the relations between Jack and his mother rapidly deteriorated. Some of Roberta's co-workers believed that Roberta was getting tired of always doing for Jack; that the idea of caring for her adult son was fine in the abstract, but when it was a daily drill, it began to pale.

"She was changing toward the end," a Safeway co-worker recalled later. "She was getting more into herself."

That meant, to some, that Roberta was beginning to make some demands on Jack—demands that he be more responsible for his own life, to consider getting his own apartment and start paying his own bills, rather than depend on his mother for everything.

Apart from her suspicions of Jack, there was the matter of Jack's lifestyle. As Bea Kennedy recalled, Jack was supposed to pay Roberta rent, to help make up for the loss of Tim's payments. But Jack failed to do this, instead spending money on compact discs, tapes, and even worse from Roberta's perspective, on dates with a married woman.

"Roberta was very unhappy," Bea recalled. "He moved in, and he's just like a little teenager. He wasn't responsible for anything. It was like he thought he was a high school kid again." Roberta complained to Bea that Jack was as irresponsible as Elmore. Bea believed that Roberta had told Jack she was kicking him out.

That was also the impression of a former Safeway employee named Carol Marino, a longtime friend of Roberta's, who in the last week of February visited from her home in Montana.

Marino had known both Roberta and Jack for 20 years. From her observation, it did not appear that they were getting along very well. There was a definite tension. It seemed to Marino that Roberta had told Jack to move; there may have been discussion about the rent Jack was supposed to be paying Roberta but wasn't.

For his part, according to Marino's observation, Jack was highly abusive verbally to Roberta. At one point, in fact, Roberta was having a conversation with Marino, and Jack overheard a portion of it; he was sure Marino and Roberta were talking about him and he became very angry.

During her week's stay with Roberta, Marino talked about Jeremy and Ashley's deaths with Jack. Jack told Marino that he wasn't a very good single parent, and that it had been easier to take care of Ashley after Jeremy's death. Jack added that maybe it was better that Jeremy died because it made it easier to take of Ashley alone, Marino said later.

By Saturday, February 25, Marino was ready to leave. Roberta, who had been on vacation, was due to return to work the following day, Sunday, February 26, 1995. As it happened, it was to be Roberta's last day on earth.

Twenty-nine

Exactly what transpired that night between Roberta Butler and Jack Barron may never be known.

Certainly it appears that Jack himself was to provide inconsistent statements of the events of the evening, if Solano County Deputy Coroner Loveless' report is to be believed. Jack told Loveless that he last had contact with his mother at 10 P.M., "over the telephone." Yet he would later say that he was asleep when Roberta came home, and that she and he had a brief face-to-face conversation before Roberta went up to her room, and Jack went back to sleep.

There was evidence that Roberta never made it to bed herself before she died; the papers on her bed seemed to show that, along with the fact that she was still in her robe when she was found the following day.

Afterward, Bea Kennedy formed a guess as to what might have happened.

Roberta, said Bea, knew about Reiber's cause of death on Ashley: "homicidal violence cannot be excluded." And Roberta certainly believed that Ashley had died on Elmore's birthday, a Sunday; that Jeremy had died on Sunday, the seventh of January; and that Irene may have died on a Sunday, the seventh of June.

All of these sevens and Sundays, Bea came to believe, may have coalesced in Roberta's mind in the weeks before her death. And in the heat of a dispute with Jack that night, Bea reasoned, it was perfectly possible that Roberta might have angrily confronted Jack with her suspicions of his guilt.

"I think," Bea said later, "that she confronted him with it." And having heard his own true believer, his most loyal supporter, his mother, tell him she believed he was guilty of murder, Jack may have decided that he now had to kill Roberta as well, Bea came to believe.

Similar thoughts ran through John Paget's mind as well, although he did not hear of Roberta's death for some time.

"There's been a lot of speculation, by myself and my immediate family," John recalled, "over what Roberta must have been thinking by the time Ashley died. I mean, on the one hand, you've got this woman who has doted over this son of hers who never did grow up. She would go to any ends of the earth to help him and do anything she could for him.

"Yet, by the time Ashley died, she had to have had some thoughts that she probably tried to repress. And I've often wondered if she ever confronted Jack or asked the question, 'Is there anything here I need to know?'

"And the one thing that gives me a chill every time I think about it, is that, is there is a moment of realization in Roberta's life, right before the end of that life, when she suddenly, when she's being held down and suffocated and asphyxiated, is realizing, *This is what happened to Ashley, and Jeremy, and Irene.* Just a flash of a moment. And it just boggles my mind each time I think about it.

"What a horrifying thing must have gone through her mind, with her own child. And especially if, as would be natural, a mother wants to repress those thoughts . . ."

BENICIA, CALIFORNIA

February 27, 1995

Thirty

Patrolman Tom Dalby, the first officer on the scene at Roberta's condominium, watched as the body removal service wheeled Roberta's bagged remains out of the condo. On the way to the van, the gurney collapsed, spilling Roberta's body to the ground.

Dalby had been a cop in Benicia for 13 years, and nothing like this had ever happened to him before. *Hell*, he thought, *this wasn't even supposed to be my call.* The patrol boundaries had just changed, but the dispatcher had forgotten, and had given the call to Dalby anyway.

Dalby tried to consider what to do next. He had most of the basic information for his report, but based on what Jack had just told him, that wasn't going to be enough information, not by a long shot. Dalby decided to go back to the Police Department and fill in the supervisor of the department's small detective section, Lt. Steve Mortensen.

Mortensen listened to Dalby's description of the scene and the brief account of the Barron family history and immediately realized that the whole situation bore looking into further. He called in one of his detectives, Monty Castillo. Mortensen told Castillo to verify Dalby's information by calling Sacramento authorities.

Around 4 P.M. that afternoon, Castillo called the Sacramento Sheriff's Department for information about Jack Barron. Someone there routed Castillo to the Sheriff's homicide unit, which in turn referred Castillo to the Sacramento County Coroner's Office.

Bob Bowers took the call.

Had Bowers ever heard of a family called Barron? Castillo asked.

Guillot was off the day Roberta was found dead, and so missed the telephone call from Castillo. But when he reported to work the following day, one of the secretaries in the Coroner's Office asked him if he'd heard the news.

"What news?" Billy asked.

Jack Barron's mother had been found dead in bed, the secretary told Guillot.

If Guillot had believed before this that Jack was a murderer, he was now absolutely certain. There was positively no way any genetic predisposition to illness—at least any shared by Irene, Jeremy and Ashley—could have been responsible for Roberta's death, since she and Irene had completely different genes.

By this time, Bowers had already sent a complete package on the three Barron deaths to the Benicia Police Department; even before this, Castillo had been in contact with the Solano County Coroner's Office, and had told them that three other members of Jack Barron's family had been found dead under mysterious circumstances, and that in at least one of the cases, Ashley's, Sacramento authorities had ruled that homicide could not be excluded as a manner of death.

Guillot talked briefly to the Solano County Coroner's Office, and was in turn referred to Castillo in Benicia. Castillo was at this point cautious in dealing with Guillot, saying that he was just beginning to investigate, and that it was too soon to form any conclusions.

Guillot now returned to the file on Irene and noticed

something he had overlooked before. There, at the top of Dr. Schmunk's autopsy report, dictated more than two long years before, was the notation:

"The body is identified by a Coroner's tag #92-1930 present at the left great toe. In addition, photographs are taken under my direction for identification purposes."

But there were no photographs in the file, other than those taken at the scene.

What happened to the photographs taken by Schmunk during the autopsy?

Guillot massaged the Coroner's records system, and after a bit of sleuthing, learned that while the film had been processed, no prints from the autopsy had ever been made. A bit more detective work on Guillot's part, and the film negatives were unearthed. Guillot ordered a complete set of the autopsy photographs, and sat back, waiting to see what they told.

Even as Guillot was rummaging around in the past, Castillo was measuring Jack. Castillo had asked Jack to come to the police station for a formal interview on the day after the discovery of Roberta's body.

Castillo was just about Jack's age, 33. He was short, dark-haired, compactly built and mild-mannered. Before joining the police department as a police aide in 1988, he had worked as a sales representative for a heating and air conditioning company. In 1991 he had joined the department as a full-time, sworn officer, and had become a detective just a few years later.

Castillo told Jack this would be a voluntary statement on his part, for background purposes, and that he would be free to leave any time he wanted to. Did Jack want to discuss his mother's death?

Of course, Jack said.

Castillo turned on a tape recorder and told Jack he would record the interview. Jack agreed to this as well.

The transcript of this interview was withheld by Benicia

Police for legal reasons, but the gist of Castillo's questions and Jack's answers was later to emerge in a court proceeding.

Castillo began by asking Jack the last time he had had any contact with Roberta.

Jack told Castillo that Sunday night had been his mother's first day back at work, and that she had worked at the Safeway from 1 P.M. to 10 P.M. Jack said he heard his mother come home around 10:15 P.M. He was sleeping when Roberta came home, Jack said.

Roberta then came down the stairs to his room, and they talked for a few minutes, Jack told Castillo. After this short conversation, Roberta went upstairs to her room. That was the last time he saw his mother alive, Jack said.

What did you do next? Castillo asked.

I went back to bed, Jack said.

Did you get up at any time during the night?

I got up about midnight to go to the bathroom. Then I made a telephone call to see whether I was scheduled to work the next morning.

What time did you get up?

I set the alarm for 4:30.

When did you leave the house?

About five. I was supposed to be at work at six.

Castillo asked Jack whether he had seen his mother at any time between 10:20 or so and five in the morning.

No, Jack said.

Did you lock the door when you left? (Castillo at this point had no idea of how compulsive Jack was about locks.)

Yes.

Castillo asked Jack where he worked, and Jack told him about the new job as the assistant conductor for Amtrak. He'd left work about 1:30 P.M., Jack said, and had gotten home quickly because the traffic was light.

Castillo asked Jack whether anything had been disturbed at the house when he returned from work; Jack said everything looked just as it had been when he left that morning.

Was the door still locked?

Yes, it was.

What did you do next?

I unlocked the door and went in and looked around, and I called out for my mother. No one answered. So I went up to her bedroom and looked inside, and that's where I found her.

After a brief discussion in which Jack told Castillo that he had noted the disturbed waterbed railing and the papers, as well as his mother's body, Castillo asked Jack about Roberta's recent health.

To Castillo, Jack ran down the usual—Roberta had been suffering from a cold; from headaches; from stress.

What kind of stress? Castillo asked.

There were problems in Roberta's union, Jack said, some sort of squabble among different factions. Roberta was on one side of the argument, and feelings had been running high.

Jack wanted to know when the authorities would release his mother's body. He had people to call and a funeral to arrange.

Soon, Castillo promised, soon. Just as soon as we can find out what killed her.

At that moment, Solano County forensic pathologist Dr. Brian L. Peterson was attempting to determine exactly that. Roberta's body lay on a shiny aluminum table in the Solano County morgue in Fairfield, California, a few miles north of Benicia, still clad in her pink bathrobe. Peterson noticed two small gold metal angels pinned to the upper left lapel of Roberta's robe—one for Jeremy, the other for Ashley.

By this time, of course, Peterson was at least basically aware of what had happened in Sacramento County and knew that authorities there suspected that each of the Barrons had been murdered. Whether those suspicions influenced Peterson in his findings on Roberta is difficult to say with certainty, although there likely was some, even if unconscious, influence. After all, Peterson knew that four unexplained deaths in one family was stretching the laws of probability.

Peterson almost immediately noticed a light red abrasion, about an inch and a half long, on Roberta's nose. A series of petechial hemorrhages could be seen on the lower left eyelid, but Peterson thought these might have been due to post-mortem lividity. It was inside Roberta's mouth that Peterson found more compelling evidence: Roberta's entire lower inner lip was marked by a light red abrasion as much as half-an-inch wide—an indication that someone had held a pillow over Roberta's face, causing her to bite through her own lip.

In his internal examination, Peterson found "numerous" petechial hemorrhages over the upper right lung. When Peterson removed Roberta's brain he discovered a prominent hemorrhage within the left mastoid bone, a finding that almost always was consistent with asphyxial death.

Three days later, Peterson signed his final report for the Solano County Coroner's Office:

"Cause of death: Asphyxia due to smothering. Manner of death: homicide," he wrote.

Peterson's conclusion was kept confidential to all but police and prosecutors, however. Officially, Roberta's death would be classified as under investigation for the next two months to give investigators room to maneuver.

On the same day, a memorial service for Roberta was held at her church in Benicia. This time there was no coffin, open or closed, because the authorities refused to release Roberta's body pending further tests.

Afterward, Bea, her husband Patrick, Tim O'Keefe and his sister Maryann, Roberta's sister Jeanne Dillon, and Roberta's mother, Edith Mitchell, shared a lunch with Jack and Roberta's priest, Father Daniel, at an Italian restaurant in old town Benicia.

The gathering was somber. Bea formed the impression

that Jeanne and Edith felt uncomfortable being around Jack.

"I can see there was something there," Bea recalled later, "like they didn't like being there with him."

Jack himself was acting strangely, Bea thought.

"I actually was kind of scared at that point," she recalled, "because we didn't live too far from where Roberta lived. He couldn't look at us. I felt that he was acting guilty, and that he felt very uncomfortable being there."

It was Bea and Tim who had made most of the memorial service arrangements, Bea recalled; again, Jack was playing the griever to the hilt. Tim was extremely angry with Jack; he'd had to find out about Roberta's death from his sister, a good friend of Roberta's.

Then Jack said something that troubled both Tim and Bea immensely.

Jack, describing his experience at finding his mother dead, told the group that Roberta had looked just like Irene.

How could that be? Tim wondered. He'd been at the Southbreeze house with Roberta, and he knew for a fact that the police had not allowed Jack into the house to see Irene's body. Bea knew that was the case as well.

Afterward, Bea and Tim discussed the situation. Jack's casual, feel-sorry-for-me remark seemed ominous. Both Bea and Tim decided to contact the police.

SACRAMENTO, CALIFORNIA
BENICIA, CALIFORNIA
March, 1995

Thirty-one

The death of Roberta Butler and the Solano County Coroner's finding of homicide galvanized the Sacramento authorities as the previous deaths of Irene, Jeremy, and Ashley had not. To Sheriff's Detective Maryl Lee Cranford, the finding of death by smothering explained almost everything.

Cranford first heard about Roberta Butler's death on the day Benicia detective Castillo called to ask about the Barrons. Cranford was out when the call came in, and when she returned someone in the department told her the news. She called Castillo to find out what was going on.

Although police agencies are often notoriously guarded about the information they share with other departments, that seems not to have been the case in the relations between the Benicia and the Sacramento departments.

Castillo filled Cranford in on his interview with Jack, while Cranford told Castillo about some of the work she and Guillot from the Sacramento Coroner's Office had done so far.

From that point forward, each department pursued its own independent investigation—Cranford on the cases of Irene, Jeremy, and Ashley, and Castillo on Roberta—but remained in frequent communication over the months that followed. Eventually, officials from both departments, joined by representatives from the coroner's offices and district attorneys of both counties, and by the State Department of Justice's Mike Prodan, were to form a multi-agency task force to share findings and strategies for the investigation of Jack Barron.

Cranford's immediate task was to build on the work previously done by Guillot. That meant tracking down people who had known the Barrons and conducting interviews; the idea was to develop a portrait of Jack's behavior before and after the deaths, and most important, to determine a theory as to how and when he might have committed the murders.

One thing was apparent to Cranford from the outset: each of the deaths held certain commonalities. In addition to the Sundays and possibly the sevens, in three of the four deaths Jack had not been present when the victim was discovered. Moreover, except in the case of Roberta, someone other than Jack had made the discovery. To Cranford, that indicated the possibility of planning ahead.

The first question to be resolved was the approximate time each death had occurred. The question was: was it possible to prove that Jack had been present at the time of death? Cranford met with Reiber and reviewed the autopsy findings once again.

Reiber pointed to Irene's liver temperature as taken by Schmunk on the morning her body was discovered as a key piece of information. If the human body cooled at a rate of one-half degree per hour, that seemed to suggest that Irene might have died well before Jack left for work on the night of June 7, 1992.

Reiber's review of Irene's file suggested to him that Irene's death most likely occurred 15 ½ hours before Reiber took the liver temperature at 10:30 A.M., plus or minus three hours. That meant the earliest time death could have taken place was at 4:30 P.M. the afternoon before, and the latest at about 10 P.M.

What had Jack told the EMTs and police? Jack had said

he'd left for work at 11 P.M. That meant, if Reiber was right about the latest time of Irene's death, Jack would have had to have been home when it took place. It didn't seem very likely that Irene had died without Jack noticing.

As for Jeremy's death, the evidence appeared to indicate that the death had taken place fairly close to the time of discovery. Since Jeremy had been discovered by the baby-sitter, Jennifer Walters, Cranford decided to go see her.

Jennifer by now was a college student. She vividly remembered the events surrounding Jeremy's death. She told Cranford how she had arrived at the Southbreeze house about 12:45 P.M., and how no one appeared to be home. She'd returned to her own home, Walters recalled, and then called Jack to see what was up. Jack had told her, Walters told Cranford, that he'd probably been in the shower when she'd first arrived.

Cranford questioned Walters about what she had observed at the Southbreeze house. Walters recalled that she had seen Jeremy apparently asleep in bed. She hadn't physically checked him at the time, only looked at him from the doorway. It was only when, two hours later, when Jeremy apparently hadn't moved an inch that Walters knew something was wrong.

Cranford thought Walters' information significant. *I'll bet that Jack was killing Jeremy even while Jennifer was ringing the doorbell the first time,* she thought. Then he went to bed, waiting for his teenage baby-sitter to make the gruesome discovery. Was that why he had told Jennifer not to let the children sleep more than three hours?

Cranford continued conducting interviews. Particularly helpful were the EMTs from the Florin fire district, who were able to describe Jack's behavior during each of the deaths. One EMT recalled something weird: after Ashley had died, Jack had dropped by the fire station to invite all the firefighters to Ashley's funeral.

Still, there appeared to be a problem with Ashley's death. In that case, both Jack and the baby-sitter, Jill Presley, were in agreement that Jack had left at 11 P.M. to go to work. Presley had told the EMTs that she'd seen Ashley in one position about midnight, and in another position when she was found dead at 4 A.M. That seemed to leave Jack out of the picture entirely.

Unless, she thought, Jack had somehow left work during the night, had driven home, killed Ashley while Presley was asleep, and then returned to work. But was that possible? Wouldn't someone have noticed Jack's absence?

Cranford decided to go to the Lucky's Supermarket Jack had been working at the night Ashley died. The store was in Woodland, northwest of Sacramento—which would have meant a 70-mile round trip for Jack. If this had happened, Jack would have had to have been missing from work for more than an hour.

At the supermarket, Cranford talked to the manager and learned that Jack had clocked in around midnight. As far as the manager could discern, Jack had been at the store until some time past 4 A.M., when he was notified of Ashley's death. But the manager agreed that it was possible that Jack might have left for some portion of the shift, because no one was monitoring his movements at all times.

Cranford decided to find Jill Presley.

Meanwhile, in Benicia, Detective Castillo and his colleagues were doing much the same thing as Cranford. Castillo talked to Roberta's neighbors to see if anything unusual had happened that day.

Margaret Hawes, for instance, remembered two things. She'd known Roberta for many years, and both women were good friends. Generally, Hawes said, Roberta was an early riser. She made it a habit to open the blinds shortly after getting up. Yet on the day Roberta was found dead, the blinds had never been opened.

And, Hawes added, when her tax accountant arrived around 10 A.M., Roberta did not telephone to see if everything was all right; usually, if someone visited either of them, Hawes said, the other called to make sure everything was okay.

What that suggested, of course, was that Roberta was dead before sunrise.

What time had Jack said he left for work? Castillo checked Jack's statements to Dalby. Jack had said he'd set his alarm for 4:30 A.M., and that he was on his way to work by five. The sun did not rise until about 6:45 A.M. on the day Roberta was found dead. If Roberta was usually up by 7 A.M., that meant her killer would have had only two hours to kill her, and in any case would have had to have had a key.

That is, Castillo thought, *assuming it wasn't Jack.*

Thirty-two

John Paget was at his office in Fallbrook when he received a telephone call from his father. It was shortly after the memorial service. Jack Paget had astonishing news: Roberta had been found dead in her bed. Tim O'Keefe had called Jack and Norma to tell them because Jack wasn't up to it.

"I hadn't even known that Tim and Roberta had split up," John recalled. "Now Tim is telling my dad that Roberta has died."

Of course, by this point, John was certain that his brother-in-law was a murderer. Now it seemed to John that Jack had killed his own mother.

John called the Benicia Police Department and was connected to Castillo.

"I wanted to make sure they had all the information, about what had already happened," he said. Despite having had some sporadic contact with Billy Guillot, at this point John had never talked to a single person from the Sacramento Sheriff's Department. He wanted to make sure that the Sacramento people hadn't dropped the ball again, and failed to notify the Benicia investigators of the Barron family history.

Castillo was very interested in talking to John. As a result, John immediately flew to Oakland, rented a car, and drove to Benicia to meet with Castillo personally.

It did not take Maryl Lee Cranford very long to track down Jill Presley.

Just like Jennifer Walters with Jeremy, the death of Ashley was a vivid recollection for Jill. Despite the medical evidence indicating that Ashley had been dead for some time before Jill found her, Jill held herself responsible for Ashley's death.

In an emotional interview, punctuated by tears, Jill told Cranford that she'd checked on Ashley shortly after Jack left to go to work; she estimated the time at about 10:30 P.M. She checked a second time around midnight, Jill said. When she looked in on Ashley from the doorway of her room, the child was lying on her right side, with the bedsheet up over a portion of her body. But when she'd awakened around 4 A.M., and checked again, Ashley was lying on her back, her pajama top had been pulled up, and the sheet pulled down.

At that point, Presley told Cranford, she'd entered the room and put her hand on Ashley's stomach, only to find it hard and cold. When she looked at Ashley's back, it appeared to be bruised. It was only later that Jill realized this was lividity.

Jill told Cranford that she blamed herself for Ashley's death, primarily because she fell asleep, despite Jack's express instructions to stay awake.

But as Jill began to describe the events of that night, alarm bells began to sound in Cranford's head.

"She told me about several unusual things Jack did that night," Cranford was to recall.

By now, Cranford had learned of Jack's obsession with making sure things were locked.

"Jack was a compulsive door locker," Cranford recalled. "He was known to drive miles back to where he started, just to be sure the doors were really locked. On the night of Ashley's death, Jack told Jill to leave the sliding glass door open 'because it was hot.' "

When Jill questioned this, Jack told her the family dog, a black Labrador that once belonged to Starla Hayes, would bark if anyone entered through the open door.

And there was one other unusual thing, Jill recalled. When she got to the house, Jack had prepared a pitcher of iced tea, and he poured a glass for her. It was very strong tea, the way Jill liked it, not the way Jack usually preferred it. It was after consuming the tea on the hot night that Jill fell asleep.

That gave Cranford an idea, a way to account for how Jill might have seen Ashley in one position after Jack left for work, and in another at 4 A.M. Based on Jill's observations, Cranford came to believe that Ashley was still alive when Jack left for work around 11 P.M. But what if Jack doctored the tea with some sort of drug, something designed to make sure Jill fell asleep? That would account for why Jill had drifted off, despite Jack's instructions.

Then, when Jill was safely asleep, Jack could sneak back into the house and either kill or move Ashley, to make it look like she had died long after Jack had left for work.

That meant, perhaps, that Jack had taken a break from his job, jumped in his car, raced across town, sneaked into the house via the open sliding door, hadn't alarmed the dog, and had done whatever he did to Ashley.

One of Cranford's colleagues, Ted Verdouris, tried to test this hypothesis by driving from and to the Lucky's where Jack was working, in the city of Woodland about 35 miles away. Verdouris, driving at night, said he'd made the round trip in about 40 minutes, Cranford said later.

On reflection, however, this seems unlikely. Driving 70 miles in 40 minutes would mean that either Jack or Verdouris had to be exceeding 100 miles an hour.

Billy Guillot, however, came up with an alternative theory. Based on the undigested contents of Ashley's stomach, and the amount of lividity and rigor mortis, Guillot guessed that Ashley was dead well before Jill had arrived.

Then, Guillot theorized, Jack had shown Jill the "sleeping" Ashley from the doorway, and distracted Jill by proffering the iced tea. Jack had made the tea strong, the way Jill liked it, to mask any taste from the sedative Jack had used to doctor the tea.

After watching Jill to make sure she'd consumed the tea, Jack left for work. The time was then about 11 P.M. But rather than driving straight to work, Jack waited in the neighborhood for a few minutes until Jill fell asleep. After 15 or 20 minutes had passed, Jack entered the house by way of the open door, moved Ashley's body into another position, and then quietly slipped back to his car. Guillot guessed that Jack could have arrived in Woodland in perhaps 40 minutes, just in time to go to work.

By then, of course, the scene would be staged, and Jack would have no reason to leave his job, race at breakneck speed across town, kill Ashley, and race back. Everything necessary would be accomplished, even including the sleeping scapegoat: Jill.

But what about Jill's report of checking Ashley around midnight? Guillot came to believe that Jill was simply confused about the time, and, still feeling guilty for having fallen asleep, had pushed ahead the time of her check to around midnight.

If that was so—if Jill felt guilty—it seemed entirely unfair, if indeed Jack *had* doctored the tea to make her fall asleep. Especially when, in November of 1994, only two months after Ashley died, Jill had tried to kill herself.

SACRAMENTO, CALIFORNIA
BENICIA, CALIFORNIA
April, 1995

Thirty-three

As March turned into April, both teams of investigators continued to interview witnesses.

Cranford had a number of discussions with John Paget, who directed her to Denise Call. John had informed Denise the month before that now Roberta was dead. The previous fall, John asked Denise about her feelings about Jack, whether she'd ever considered the possibility that Jack had killed Ashley. Denise was glad to have someone to talk to about her suspicions.

Now, with Roberta dead, Denise came to the came conclusion as Bea Kennedy.

"My guess was," she said later, "that [Roberta] figured it out. I think she figured it out and confronted him with it." To keep his secret, Denise thought, Jack had murdered his own mother.

Denise told Cranford that she and Cliff both believed that Jack had killed all three Barrons, as well as Roberta. And Denise added something that Cranford hadn't known before: that Irene, at the end of May of 1992, had told her that she suspected Jack was having an affair with a coworker, and that she had confronted him with this.

This was interesting information to Cranford, since it

gave Jack an apparent motive for killing his wife. Cranford decided to try to find out who the co-worker was. The search did not take long before Cranford learned of Starla Hayes.

For Castillo and his colleagues in Benicia, there were two important areas that needed to be covered: Jack's movements on the day Roberta's body was discovered, and Jack's remarks about Roberta's reported stress from the union squabble.

The Solano County pathologist, Dr. Peterson, was unwilling to be pinned down on exactly when Roberta might have died. He told investigators that while it appeared to him that Roberta had definitely died less than 12 hours before she was found, it was also possible that Roberta had been dead less than six hours when Jack found her. In fact, said Peterson, it was possible (although not likely) that Roberta might have been alive right up until the time of the 911 phone call made by Jack.

This inexactitude meant there was a world of possibilities for Roberta's killer.

Was there any possibility, for example, that Roberta might have been murdered by someone connected to the union trouble? It hardly seemed likely, especially since Roberta's front door, by Jack's own account, was locked when he returned from work. Nor had Jack reported hearing anyone come in, or thrashing about in Roberta's bedroom, in the middle of the night. With the undrawn blinds, and Roberta still in her bathrobe, it seemed that the murder had to have taken place either when Jack was in the house, or in the two hours or so between the time Jack left and Roberta usually arose. Otherwise, if the murder had taken place later, why was Roberta still in her robe and the blinds still drawn?

Still, the decision was made to interview various people in the union to determine their whereabouts on the night and morning in question.

And what about Tim O'Keefe? Jack made it plain that he and Tim were not exactly the best of buddies, and that Tim and Roberta hadn't been getting along in the months just before Tim left. Was it possible that Tim had somehow slipped into the house and suffocated Roberta? Someone would have to check on Tim to make sure that hadn't happened.

Meanwhile, one detective was detailed to run down Jack's movements on February 27. The detective collected Jack's timecard from Amtrak, and interviewed Frank Klatt, the conductor. It first appeared that Klatt was with Jack from 6 A.M. until 11 A.M., when the train crew took a break. Klatt thought Jack had spent most of the break in the crew room with him and other Amtrak workers. The break lasted until about 12:30, when the crew returned to work for one more hour, until punchout time at 1:30 P.M.

That seemed to dispose of Jack's opportunity to commit the murder at any time between, say, 5:30 A.M. and 1:30 P.M.

But then Castillo learned of another resident of the condominium complex, Jessica Vasquez, who claimed that she had seen Jack in front of Roberta's condo at 12:30 in the afternoon, and again later that day a little after 2:00 P.M.

How could this be? If Klatt had seen Jack at 12:30 in Oakland, how could Vasquez see him at the same time 40 miles away, half an hour after noontime? Vasquez said she was positive it was Jack who she had seen the first time.

Castillo called Klatt back to clarify matters. This time Klatt said he'd begun working with Jack about 6:20 A.M., and was with him until 10:30 A.M. Klatt then drove his car to the passenger depot. Klatt said he saw Jack get in his van and drive off. The next time he saw Jack, Klatt said, was about 11:10 A.M. Jack got on the train with Klatt, and they arrived at the maintenance yard about 11:40.

After that, Klatt told Castillo, he did not see Jack from about 11:40 A.M. until about 12:40 or 12:50 P.M. At that time, he and Jack got on the departing train and arrived at the passenger depot at 1 P.M.

That meant Jack could have driven from Oakland to Benicia after 11:40, arrived there around 12:10 or so, killed Roberta, was seen by Vasquez at 12:30. But for this to work, it had to mean Jack then drove from Benicia to Oakland in a little over 20 minutes. That didn't seem possible.

Given all the permutations, the best solution seemed the simplest one: that Vasquez had simply been wrong about seeing Jack at 12:30; perhaps she'd seen someone who looked like Jack. Given the amount of lividity and rigor mortis present in Roberta's body, her attire, and the fact that she was apparently reading business papers when she died, everything pointed to her having been killed sometime around midnight or 1 A.M., again when Jack was in the house.

By early April, the task force investigating the Barron-Butler deaths was of two minds about the motive for the crimes: either Jack had killed his wife, children, and mother for purely psychological reasons, or he had killed them for the insurance money.

Investigators in Sacramento pieced together the payouts received for the deaths of Irene, Jeremy, and Ashley: about $41,000. It seemed difficult to believe that Jack had murdered his own family for such a relatively small amount of money; the risk-reward ratio seemed far too marginal. On the other hand, when coupled with an assumption that Jack's underlying motivation was to free himself of the responsibilities of adulthood, the insurance benefits could be construed as a side benefit: not only would Jack rid himself of his obligations, he could get paid for it at the same time.

It was when investigators considered what Jack might gain from the death of Roberta that the monetary motive came even more strongly into play.

Roberta had life insurance policies totaling nearly $130,000; in addition, she owned a condominium likely to bring in more cash if sold. It was likely that the money for

Irene, Jeremy, and possibly Ashley had already been spent; a new infusion of $130,000 in insurance alone from Roberta's policies might be ample motive for Roberta's death.

And finally, there was the question posed by Bea Kennedy: had Roberta confronted Jack with her belief that Jack killed Irene, Jeremy, and Ashley? Was that why Jack might have killed Roberta, as well—to keep her quiet?

While these investigations and speculations were proceeding, the California Department of Justice's profiler, Mike Prodan, continued his assessment of the Barron case. Now, however, Prodan had the information from the Butler death as well; the Benicia Police Department had asked Prodan to consider their case as well as those of Irene, Jeremy, and Ashley.

Afterward, Prodan's assessment of the Barron case remained confidential for legal reasons. But enough is known about the case particulars and the art of psychological profiling to hazard some guesses as to the conclusions Prodan may have come up with.

From his experience, Prodan knew that many, probably most, crimes that occurred out of psychological motivations required some sort of trigger—usually some form of stress. A crying child, an intense argument with a spouse, some event that painfully demonstrated a perpetrator's inadequacy. These were the sorts of stresses that could trigger a psychologically motivated homicidal event. Based on what he had learned from both the Benicia and Sacramento investigators, it was likely that Jack was susceptible to a number of stresses.

One, perhaps, was the occasion of Elmore's birthday, a Sunday, August 7, 1938. It was possible that the significance of a Sunday the seventh was sufficient to remind Jack of his own unhappy relationship with his departed father, leading to a generalized anxiety, irritation, and sensitivity. All that would be required to ignite the explosion would be some event that might illustrate Jack's inadequacy or lack of control over his environment. An argument with Irene, perhaps; or maybe wild, recalcitrant behavior by Jeremy; either might serve to motivate Jack to rid his life of these irritations. Certainly Jack's obsession with cleanliness and order seemed to indicate a willingness to jettison anything he might consider an unwanted encumbrance, if it was too messy.

For Ashley, Jack's anxiety about being a single parent, coupled with his delusions about a future with Wynonna Judd, may have precipitated a desire to be free of obligations; his behavior after moving in with Roberta—his reported unwillingness to pay rent, to ignore his mother's demands and criticisms—seems akin to a teenager rebelling against adult burdens.

In any event, by early April, Prodan had developed a plan for investigators to use in interrogating Jack. The object was to induce Jack to admit to being responsible for the deaths of his mother, wife, and children. The key was to play upon Jack's apparent intense narcissism—his self-centeredness, using his own exaggerated feelings of being a tragic victim.

"We wanted to play on his self-pity," Cranford recalled of Prodan's recommendations. "We wanted to give him an out, by letting him blame these crimes on the problems his father and mother caused him."

That, at least, was the carrot employed in Prodan's plan: to validate Jack's sense of being wronged, of being one of the victims. But there was another side, as well: prepped by Prodan, the investigators were prepared to confront Jack with certainty—the hard fact that murder had been committed, and the inevitable truth that it had to be Jack who was the murderer.

With this two-pronged approach, the task force hoped to crack Jack's self-image and drive him into his habitual comfort zone of feeling sorry for himself.

On April 17, both sets of investigators were in Benicia

for the long-planned interrogation. Castillo asked Jack to come to the Benicia Police Station, and said his department had just a few questions they needed to resolve before they could officially release Roberta's body for burial.

The entire interview, lasting more than five hours, was surreptitiously videotaped. First up in the questioning were Monty Castillo and Al Garza, an investigator for the Solano County District Attorney's Office. It would be Castillo and Garza's job to soften Jack up by directly confronting him. Waiting in the wings with the carrot would be Sacramento's Cranford and Verdouris. Present to advise both teams was the Department of Justice's Prodan.

Thirty-four

Jack entered the interview room seemingly quite relaxed and in an apparently cooperative mood. The general impression he projected was of someone more than willing to help the police answer any unresolved questions.

Castillo got the ball rolling.

"Before we get started," Castillo said, "I just wanted to thank you for coming down here. I know it's been a tough month and a half for you, we understand that. We just have a few things we needed to clear up regarding the report, and regarding some details we didn't have before. Now, at any time, if you feel like leaving, you're free to go, at any time."

Jack nodded that he understood, and seated himself in a chair. Jack crossed his right ankle over his left knee and gazed calmly at Castillo.

Castillo deliberately did not give Jack a warning against self-incrimination, the Miranda warning, because Jack was not in custody.

Castillo now referred to Jack's earlier statement of February 28, the day after Roberta died.

"Do you want to add anything to that?" Castillo asked.

"Not that I can think of," Jack said.

Castillo asked if Jack was sure he had nothing to add, and Jack again said no.

"There's a lot of things we don't understand about your mother's death," Castillo said, "and you're the only one who can help us out. We've completed the investigation into the death of your mother, and what this investigation reveals is that your mother did not die of natural causes."

"What are you getting at?" Jack asked.

"It was the direct result of somebody harming your mother," Castillo said. "The investigation revealed that your mother died of being asphyxiated. The investigation, what it's telling us, on completion, is that your mother was smothered to death."

Those watching observed Jack intently. This was the moment, if Jack was innocent, for him to grow excited and stand up and demand an explanation from Castillo: What did Castillo mean, saying Roberta was murdered? Who did it? Why?

Or, alternatively, to ask how Castillo was so sure that smothering was the cause of death. Or even, to make for the door, telling Castillo that he had nothing further to say, and to call his lawyer.

But Jack did and said nothing. He continued to gaze at Castillo, apparently unperturbed.

Castillo tried once more.

"Like I said before, the autopsy report is very, very clear, that your mother did die at the hands of another. It was not natural. And the injuries were caused by another person."

Still Jack sat quietly. Castillo shifted gears to a more direct approach.

"Mr. Barron," he said, "now is the time, if you had anything to do with your mother's death, now is the time to tell us, right now."

Jack for the first time appeared startled.

"You mean me?" he asked. He laughed.

"I'm asking you, Mr. Barron."

"No," Jack said.

Castillo tried again.

"Now is the time to make something good, to try to make something good, out of a terrible situation that happened to your mother," he said.

For the first time, Jack displayed some irritation.

"What are you implying here?" he asked.

"I want to know, we'd like to know, if you had anything to do with your mother's death," Castillo said.

"No, I did not," Jack said, firmly. Still Jack made no move to terminate the interview, or ask whether Castillo intended to arrest him, since Castillo seemed to believe that Jack had killed Roberta.

"Because now is the time to tell us," Castillo added.

"I had nothing to do with my mother's death," Jack said.

"Okay," said Castillo. "Mr. Barron, who could have done something like this?"

"I have no idea."

"What's your take on something like this?"

"I don't know," Jack said.

Castillo tried to start over, in an obvious attempt to elicit some sort of reaction from Jack other than a blanket denial. The idea was to get Jack to start talking, and so far, nothing was working.

"The conclusion of the investigation revealed to us that you are responsible for your mother's death," Castillo said. "This month-and-a-half, this extensive investigation that the Benicia Police Department has done, along with [the Solano County District Attorney's Office], along with the Department of Justice, along with the Attorney General's Office, all of this information and these resources that we've added to, in the last month and a half, in a very, very extensive investigation . . . revealed that you are responsible for the death of your mother."

Castillo was now trying to impress on Jack that it wasn't just Castillo who was of the opinion that Jack killed Roberta, but a host of other law enforcement officials as well. Sometimes this worked to make a suspect feel hopeless in continuing a denial.

But Jack wouldn't succumb.

"No, I'm not," he said, simply and directly.

It was as if Castillo were deaf to Jack's denials. He tried appealing to Jack's vanity.

"What myself and Investigator Garza want to know is how such a very bright and intelligent man like yourself could have planned this? This is the most extensive investigation we've ever done."

"I didn't do it," Jack said again.

Again Castillo ignored Jack.

"So the only question we have, Mr. Barron, is, we know you did it. That is not the question. The question myself and Investigator Garza have is, why? How did you do it?"

Garza broke in at this point.

"We just want to understand, basically, you know, why? Why somebody like you would do something like this?"

Garza, a muscular man who favored tooled cowboy boots and a flowing mustache, and who could be intimidating, now perched himself on the edge of a desk and stared at Jack.

Jack saw that he was expected to give some sort of extended response beyond a simple "I didn't do it."

"I loved my mother very much," Jack said, displaying some emotion for the first time. "She has been there for me over a lot of tragic times. I wouldn't do that. Where do you guys get off saying that?"

Jack appeared to splutter with indignation. To those watching, it seemed somehow feigned—outrage for outrage's sake.

"This is," Jack said, "this is an absolute nightmare. I don't believe this." He sat up straighter, and glared at the two detectives.

Now everyone watching expected Jack to go for the door, to tell Garza and Castillo that the interview was over.

Instead, Jack settled back in his chair and resumed his gaze at Garza.

Garza picked up Peterson's autopsy report and flipped through its five pages.

"It says she died at the hands of another," Garza told Jack. "We need to understand, [because] along with the rest of the investigation, [it] says it all comes back to [no-body] else but you. What we want to know is, [what] we need [is], the answers to those questions."

"I didn't do it," Jack said one more time.

Garza tried a different approach.

"You have no idea who you think may have done it?" he asked.

"No," said Jack.

"How about who do you think might have done it?"

"I know I talked with her around that time they were having some problems in her union over in Vallejo," Jack said.

"The union?"

"Yeah," Jack said.

"The union had nothing to do with it," Garza said.

Jack shook his head at this information, and asked Garza if he believed that just because the union wasn't involved, that meant it had to be Jack?

"Mr. Barron, let me explain something to you," Castillo said. "During this investigation I got to talk with a lot of union members, okay? Your mother supported Pete Roswell, correct?"

"Right," Jack said.

Castillo shook his head. He went through a number of names of people involved in the union dispute, and told Jack that he'd done a thorough investigation of each one.

"We found their whereabouts during the time of the death of your mother," Castillo said. "They've all been alibied. And it's not a possibility. Zero. Is there anybody else you think might have done it?"

"All right, fine," Jack said, accepting Castillo's assertion that no one in the union could have been involved.

"Is there anybody else you think might have done it?" Castillo asked.

"No," Jack said.

Garza now tried to induce Jack to talk about his relations with Roberta, and asked him what he and Roberta had fought about.

"Minor stuff, you know," Jack said.

Garza asked Jack whether Roberta had ever made Jack mad enough for him to want to kill her.

Once more Jack showed some emotion.

"Of course not," he said. "Absolutely not."

"Well, what were the things you fought about?" Garza asked.

Jack muttered something no one could make out. Garza prompted him again.

"After my daughter's death, I got another good job at the railroad," Jack said. "She wanted me to move back in. I said, 'Well, you've got your own life now.' I said, 'Are you sure you want to do this?' She goes, 'Yeah.' Because at the time there was another person there. Her boyfriend."

Jack made some reference to Tim O'Keefe, but Garza persisted in asking Jack what he and Roberta had fought about.

"Oh, minor things," Jack said. "Like, you know, I'm 33 years old, and in her eyes, I'm probably still 13 or 14. You know, you never outgrow that stage," Jack meaning, in the eyes of one's mother. But it was a small thing, Jack added.

"I'd never harm my mother," he said.

"What sort of things would you argue about?" Garza persisted.

"Just petty things," Jack said. "You know. You know, she'd get wound up on certain things, and I, you know, brushed it off, no big deal. But my mom and I have been through a lot since the divorce from my biological father.

She's been there for me every time. I've been there for her on a few occasions too.

"Now, for the last three years or so, with all that's gone on, she's been solid. She's been there for me. And, uh, no, I wouldn't ever, ever do something like that to my mother."

Garza switched approaches again, inviting Jack to say, if all this was true, that Roberta and he were so close, how Jack could possibly have killed her.

"I didn't do it," Jack said, one more time.

Thirty-five

Garza tried enlisting Jack's sympathy for the investigators.

"Put yourself in our shoes," Garza told Jack. "So that we can explain it. And understand it. You can understand what we're trying to find out."

"I loved my mother very much," Jack said, and again made passing reference to Tim. Jack suggested to Garza that perhaps his mother had developed another relationship, one he did not know about.

"What you don't understand is," Garza said, ignoring the opening about Roberta's possible other relationships, "we're not trying to take anything away from you, in the sense that you loved your mom.

"I truly believe you did. I mean, you do. That's not the issue here. I don't want to debate that because I fully believe you. I'm not saying—we have not said that you don't love your mom. That's not the issue."

It was just that, Garza said, the investigators believed Jack knew more about Roberta's death than he was saying.

"No I don't," said Jack.

"Sure you do. You found her. How can we explain your mom's death? How would you explain it to us?"

"I have no idea."

"Can you give it a try? I mean, just try it."

"Why don't I tell you how it happened, or whatever you're expecting? I went to work. I came home. I can't tell you any more than that. I'm sorry. I was ill that week."

"There are two theories," Garza said, again ignoring Jack's denial. "One from our captain here in the Benicia Police Department, okay, he seems to think, he has no doubt that you were responsible for your mother's death, but what he believes happened, the captain, is you had planned this for a very, very long time. He's saying that you premeditated this, and killed your mother for just her money. This is what our captain is telling us."

But, said Garza, neither he nor Castillo agreed with the Benicia captain; they believed, they told Jack, that Jack killed Roberta because Roberta had done something bad to him.

"She had already wrongly accused you of something you did not do," Castillo said, hearkening back to the days of Elmore and Roberta. "This is the way Investigator Garza and myself feel. What we feel now is that during that conflict, at the time, you just lost control. Lost control of yourself. And when you lose control, you hurt your mother. Which resulted in your mother dying, in that conflict. We don't think you're a premeditated killer. Not at all."

Castillo again praised Jack for his intelligence.

"Which way is it, Mr. Barron?" Castillo persisted.

"I'm sorry," Jack said, shaking his head to indicate that neither theory was true, because he hadn't done it.

"What happened?" Garza persisted. "She made you so angry that you just couldn't hold it in check anymore?"

"Nope," Jack said.

"Something happened, okay?" Garza said. "Something did happen."

Now Garza got up and moved closer to Jack, staring at him intensely.

"Something happened," Garza said.

Jack said nothing.

"Something happened."

Again Jack kept silent.

"Something happened," Garza repeated, his eyes boring in on Jack's. "She's the one who made you angry. She did something to you."

Jack finally appeared to get angry.

"How can I tell you what happened when I wasn't there?" he said, raising his voice.

"After all this investigation, there's no doubt in anybody's mind, Mr. Barron, that you did it," Garza said.

The interrogation ground on, with Garza and Castillo laboring to induce Jack to confess. Jack continued to insist that he had nothing to do with Roberta's death.

"I didn't kill my mother. I didn't do this," Jack said.

"Your mother didn't suffer," Castillo offered. "It wasn't a brutal death. You just happened to lose control. Which resulted in the death of your mother. She didn't suffer. She didn't suffer at all. There's no question in our minds at all, that you did not want you mother to suffer. So which one was it?"

Jack shook his head, but did not reply.

"Why should we believe you're not responsible?" Garza demanded.

"I had a lot of respect and admiration for my mother."

"I'm not knocking that," Garza said. "I understand that. But I still believe that you did it. Mr. Barron, tell me why we shouldn't believe you didn't do it."

"I didn't do it."

"But you did. We believe you did. We just want to understand the reason behind it. Why should we believe you didn't do it?"

Jack sighed, but said nothing.

"We already know, Mr. Barron. We are not trying to convince you of anything," Garza said. "We are already convinced.

"Mr. Barron," Garza said, attempting to compel Jack to

look at him directly. "We're not trying to make you do anything. Okay? What we'd like is for you to convince me that you didn't do it. That's all I'm asking."

"I didn't do it."

"We believe you did it."

"You believe?"

"We believe."

"No, there's no question," Castillo said. "We know you did it. We just have that question of why. On why, we want you to help us out."

After almost an hour, the interrogation had degenerated into repetition, with the investigators confronting Jack over and over with their belief that he was a killer, and Jack doggedly persistent in his denials. The object now was to wear Jack down, engage his emotions, spark some incautious response on his part that could provide an opening wedge. If Jack decided to leave, the investigators had Plan B ready to go.

By about 4:30 in the afternoon, Jack was visibly tired; so were Castillo and Garza. Yet Jack stuck steadfastly to his story, like a fighter on the ropes who wouldn't go down.

Garza told Jack that the police believed Roberta had accused him of being like Elmore. That he was irresponsible. That he was fooling around with a married woman. It wasn't his fault, Garza told Jack; Roberta had just pushed his button, and he'd lost control. It was Roberta's fault, really, Garza told Jack.

Wearily, Jack said it wasn't true.

Garza asked Jack if he'd blacked out during the murder. Jack said he hadn't even been there. Garza confronted Jack with the statement from the witness, Jessica Vasquez, and said it proved Jack was lying.

"You lied," Garza said. "There's nobody else but you. Nobody else, Jack. Not Tim, not the union. There's nobody else but Jack. Nope. Only Jack."

Jack said nothing to this.

"Now we've got more," Garza said. "Irene didn't die of natural causes. Irene was smothered. She died of asphyxiation."

"No, she didn't," Jack said. "The Coroner's report said it was undetermined causes."

Garza shook his head.

"That was then, this is now. Okay, Jack? This may take awhile to get to the truth, but she died of asphyxiation. Somebody smothered her. You know this, don't you Jack?"

"No."

"Yeah, you do."

"No."

"You do. You do."

Jack shook his head. Garza appeared to lose his temper.

"God, I wish you would be honest with me!"

"I am."

"No, you're not, you're not being honest with me. You're being insulting. I'm being honest with you, but you're not being honest with me.

"Irene died of asphyxiation. She was smothered in a way that her airway was obstructed. She died at the hands of another human being. Just like Roberta died at the hands of a human being. It was not a mysterious death, it was not the Lord coming down on anybody. She died at the hands of somebody else.

"They both hurt you," Garza prompted.

"No."

"They did. There's no other explanation, Jack. I defy you to come up with one."

"I can't."

"You can. How did it happen?"

"I don't know."

"You know, Jack."

"I have no idea."

"You know. You have an idea."

"I don't know."

"You know, you're lying."

"There's nothing to tell."

"There's a lot to tell."

Garza said again that the evidence showed the only person who could possibly have killed Roberta was Jack, unless Jack could come up with someone else.

"Who would that be?" Garza prompted.

"I told you, I can't," Jack said.

"You can do better. You can do a lot better."

"I know what happened at work," Jack said. "I know what happened that day, and obviously, whatever I tell, it can't make any difference. There isn't anything I can say or do to change your mind, you're already pretty much . . ."

Jack's voice trailed off.

"You're guilty because nobody else could have done it," Garza said. "Who else got there? Who else had a key? With the house secured? By your own words, you opened up the house yourself, Jack."

"Yeah, I had a key to the house. I walked in the door . . ."

"We've been over this," Garza said. "You're the only one with a key. That's why we know it's you. You don't have any other options, with regard to giving us an idea of who could have done this. It's time, Jack.

"It was just like all those other times. It was no different. It just built up. It built up. And you choked your mom. The reason for this was she hurt you."

"I've had over my share of hurt," said Jack, "but I would never take it out on anybody."

"The hurt is over now," Garza said. "She's not going to hurt you again, is she? She's not going to be able to tell you that you're like your father. She's not going to be able to tell you that you're wasting money, that you're living in her house without paying rent, that you're messing around just like your dad with a married woman. She's not going to be able to do that anymore, is she?"

*   *   *

The interrogation dragged on. Still Jack made no move to leave.

"We don't think you're a bad guy," Garza said. "We just want to know why." But, said Garza, once it got out that police suspected him of killing Roberta and Irene, everyone was going to think he was a bad guy.

"What other people?" Jack asked.

"Everybody, Jack," Garza said. "Everybody. Everybody's going to believe you're a bad guy. Everybody's going to believe you're not that model kid that you said you were. Okay? Everybody. You name 'em. They. Will. Believe that. Don't kid yourself. Don't kid yourself with thinking that those people aren't going to believe that. It's not important what person, they're going to believe that, the important part is that everybody's going to believe that."

"I didn't kill them. I don't know what happened, or what did happen. I am not responsible for that," Jack said.

"You are, Jack, that's a fact. You are responsible for everything."

"Never."

"I don't care how many times you deny it, we're never going to change that. The fact is you are responsible for it, you did it. You injured your mother, you injured Irene, it happened. Yes it did, Jack. It's a fact. You cannot get away from it.

"You might as well face it, you know you did it. There's nobody else responsible. It's you Jack."

Jack sighed, and said nothing.

"How are we going to do this?" Garza continued. "Are you going to continue to lie? You're the only one with the opportunity to end it. So what do you think?"

Finally, after almost five hours, Jack had had enough.

"I think it's stupid," Jack said

"I don't think so," Garza said.

"Yeah," said Jack, standing up. "I'm going now."

There was a knock on the door. Castillo opened it. Cranford and Verdouris entered the room.

Jack sat down again.

Thirty-six

"You're not under arrest, you understand that? And you're free to leave at any time," Cranford told Jack, pulling a chair up directly in front of him.

Cranford seated herself within two feet of Jack's face. She reached out her right hand and put it on Jack's knee. She bent over slightly to gain eye contact with Jack, who was looking down. She adopted her most sympathetic tone.

"Mr. Barron, get something going for yourself," Cranford said. "We know about Irene, we know about Roberta, and we know who is responsible. There's only one person who's responsible, and it's time to get something going for yourself. And maybe it was medication that made you act goofy, or whatever. Otherwise, you are a very cold, calculating murderer."

Jack said nothing, but continued to gaze at the floor.

"This is the first time I ever met you," Cranford said, "but I know you from talking to many, many of your past friends and acquaintances. And I know you're hurting.

"You were on medication, isn't that right?"

Jack said he'd been taking two kinds of over-the-counter cold medicine at the time of Roberta's death.

"How did that make you feel?" Cranford asked.

"It knocks me out," Jack said.

"Before you go to sleep, you get kind of woozy?"

"Nope, I just basically hunker down, try to beat it."

"Do you drink alcohol?"

"No, not when I have a cold," Jack said. "It was one of those chest ones that you have in there, and just a persistent cough, I'd just take my shot."

"Do you think that the combination of the medicine could have made you act in a way you normally would not have acted?"

"I don't think it would have, no," said Jack. "I've had it before."

Jack went on to describe recent illnesses he had suffered. Suddenly, it was as if Jack were in a sickroom relating his recent health history to a sympathetic nurse. He talked about his knee injury, and his appendectomy. Cranford tried to steer the subject away from Jack's health complaints and back to the subject at hand.

"Something happened with Irene," Cranford said, dismissing Jack's medical history.

"Irene was asphyxiated. Something happened with Roberta. Roberta was asphyxiated, and you were responsible for that. It happened. And if you tell us it happened, you need to talk to me. Because I don't think any one of us here wants to believe that you are as cold and calculating as you appear to be right now."

Almost imperceptibly, Cranford's voice fell into a slow, steady rhythm, almost a monotone. The effect was soothing, almost hypnotic.

"I don't think you're a bad person," Cranford said. "I've talked to a lot of people. A lot of people are very, very [convinced] that Jack is not a bad person. Jack has had some trouble in his life. His father left him when he was 12 years old, and his father has gone off and married countless women since Roberta, had other children, who he spends more time with than he ever spent with you.

"And then you have Irene, accusing you. I know she

accused you of having an affair, because she talked to your mother about it. Your mother agreed. She talked to Denise about it. She told them that she planned to confront you about it.''

Jack said nothing to this, and the silence dragged on for a minute or two.

Verdouris now asked Jack what had happened when Irene confronted him with her suspicions.

Jack denied that Irene had ever doubted him.

''Why would she tell Roberta that she did?'' Cranford demanded.

Jack denied that Irene had ever said anything like that to Roberta.

''Roberta told me herself,'' Cranford said. ''Did Roberta ever tell you that she had talked to me?''

This was a bit of trickery on Cranford's part, since she had never talked to Roberta before her death. But giving Jack the impression that Cranford had been investigating him even before Roberta died might make Jack wonder whether Roberta had told Cranford anything incriminating— such as any suspicions Roberta might have had that Jack was responsible for the deaths of Irene, Jeremy and Ashley. In effect, Cranford was poking directly at whatever fears Jack might have that Roberta had told someone else of her suspicions.

Jack again heatedly denied that he had had an affair, that Irene had confronted him, and that Irene had talked to Roberta.

''I talked to Roberta,'' Cranford said again. Jack became agitated. ''Roberta told me about Irene calling her and talking about the possibility that you were having an affair. Because you were going away. And Roberta agreed. And Roberta agreed that you were being more and more like your father.''

After another silence, Cranford said, ''I don't believe you meant to hurt your wife. I know how hard it is to have a father leave his son. At that critical age. At a time when he needs that father the most. And I know you never wanted to be that kind of person.

"There are things that happen, that other people perceive, other people see things, and they start believing . . . and I don't think you ever wanted to be like that. And when someone starts telling you that you were being like that, that's a hard thing."

"He was a jerk," Jack said.

"I know that."

"It is a hard thing, yes," said Jack, "and everything, but I don't think you know how he acted."

"Jack," said Cranford, "you are the only person. You are the last person to see Irene, when you went to work. We know that she died right at that time, within half an hour or so, of your leaving for work. We have her liver temperature. There's only one way it can get that low."

Another silence ensued.

"Jack," said Cranford, "now is the time for *you*. Get something going for *you*. Because I know you care more about yourself than you're letting on. And I know that you do not want all your friends to believe that you are a cold, calculating asshole. Excuse my language. Because that's what they're going to think."

Jack seemed very close to the breaking point, Cranford thought. He continued to gaze at the floor. He was visibly agitated.

Cranford again offered the carrot.

"If there was something that was beyond your control, because of the things that happened in your life, that's an understandable thing, Jack. I work with people like this every day. You're not the first person who has had an accident. You're not the first person that something has happened in your life that you wished to take away or you wished never happened. It's not the end of your life. And the only way to go on in a positive way is to turn this around and start to get something for yourself going."

There was another pause, and Jack said nothing.

"God will forgive you," Cranford said. "God has already forgiven you, Jack. If you have come to terms and faced . . . the truth. But He will not forgive you if you're lying. Because God knows the truth. And I don't know, if you lie, how you can believe in God anymore."

Thirty-seven

Again, Cranford tried to get Jack to talk about his feelings on the night before Irene was discovered.

"How did you feel that night at work?" she asked.

"Fine, I was just concerned about Irene, that's all," Jack said.

"Knowing that she was laying there on the bed and the kids were going to find her." Cranford made it a statement, not a question.

"I didn't know any of that," Jack said. "I don't know anything I can tell you."

"Jack," Cranford said, "we know about all of it."

"All of what?"

"All of it. Irene. Roberta. Ashley. Jeremy."

Jack was silent.

"It's over, Jack," Cranford said. "You can walk out of this room right now and that's not going to change a thing. It's not going to go away. Because we're not going to go away. And Jill already told us that she did not tell the whole truth on that casualty report. She told us that you told her that you'd just checked on Ashley, and that she was okay, that she was going to sleep. She originally said she'd checked on her. We now know that she didn't. We also

212 / CARLTON SMITH

know that Ashley was suffocated shortly after she ate dinner.

"Do you remember what she had for dinner that night?"

"I didn't have her, my mom had her," Jack said.

"What time did she come home?"

"About eight. My mom put her to bed. Then I had to go to work."

"Jill came and you told her, 'I just checked on Ashley,' so there was no need to."

Verdouris broke in.

"Come on, Jack. Tell us what happened," he said.

"There isn't anything else."

"Yes there is," Cranford said.

"I didn't do it."

"Yes you did. Yes you did," Cranford said. "I know you don't feel real great about it. But at least we'd like to believe that you feel bad."

"I don't, because I loved my family, my kids and my mother," Jack said. "Everybody's putting me down to be the bad guy here."

"Jack," Cranford said, "it's not a matter of being a bad guy. I don't think you're a bad guy. That has nothing to do with it. I think that you're a good man. From everybody I've talked to, you're a good man. But there are issues in your life that you need to work out, that have caused things to happen. There are issues that stem back to when you were a child. That you have never been able to deal with. And they're coming up now. And you can't go on like this. And I don't think you'd want it to happen again."

"Tell the truth, Jack," Verdouris urged.

"The only way anybody can help you is for you to tell the truth yourself," Cranford said. "I want to get you the help you need to start dealing with some of the issues that you have bottled up inside of you, since your father left you. Probably for some time before that."

Cranford again said she thought Jack was a good man, but one who had been hurt very deeply, and that he was "working out these issues."

"Jack," she said, "it's been a long time coming. This is the only way you were taught. This is the way your father taught you. You didn't want your children to have a father who left them. You weren't going to do to them what your father did to you.

"Jack, it's time to get off this runaway train," Cranford continued. "We know about all the lies."

"What lies?"

"The lies are going to be coming home. About your being there when Roberta died. You know, checking on Ashley. About Irene suspecting you were having an affair. With every . . . lie, Jack, you're digging yourself deeper and deeper and deeper, and making yourself look worse and worse and worse. You do. To everybody, Jack. To everybody, because, you know what? Pretty soon, everybody's going to know. And you are going to look like one cold son-of-a-gun. One cold fish, unfeeling, just like that.

"And I don't think you're like that. I can see the hurt in your eyes right now," Cranford said. "Your true friends will stand by you. The only thing a true friend asks is to be honest. Just be honest. And if they're your friends, they will love you anyway. They will understand that there were things outside of Jack's control that caused Jack to do what he did."

"Jack," Verdouris interjected. "We know, but we need you to tell us why. We need to be able to understand, Jack. Help us to know. We don't know why. What was going on in your mind? Tell us what you were feeling. Tell us what you were feeling."

"I don't know how I feel right now," Jack said.

"We're not asking right now, Jack, we're asking how you felt at the time the things that caused the accident happened," Cranford said. "Unless you want me to believe that they were cold and calculated killings."

"They're not, okay?" Jack said.

"Then tell us how the accidents happened," Cranford said.

"I don't know."

"You do know, Jack. Deep in your heart. Deep in your heart, and it's not going to go away. Deep in your feelings, Jack, and it's not going to go away. It's in your brain, and it's not going to go away. You can push it to the farthest part of your mind, and wherever you go, it's always going to be there. It's going to weigh you down like a ton weight."

Jack said nothing.

"This is the way your father would be," Cranford said. "You don't care."

Jack grew agitated.

"I'm, I'm very, very irate right now," he said.

"But you do care, don't you?" Cranford asked.

"Yes, I do."

"Then get something going for you, Jack," Verdouris said. "Let's get to the bottom. What was going through Jack's mind? What was hurting Jack? Making him angry?"

"We just want to get you the help you need, so it doesn't, it isn't going to happen again," Cranford said.

"I wasn't feeling anything because I didn't do anything," Jack said.

"So you didn't feel anything?"

"I didn't feel anything of a violent nature because I didn't feel violent," Jack said.

"Jack, this was not a violent act," Cranford said.

"Well," Jack said, "these people are dead."

Cranford again probed for Jack's feelings about the deaths.

"I was just trying to get over it," Jack said, "and then a daughter, and a son, and now my ass is in a sling."

"We're trying to help you," Cranford said.

Jack didn't respond, and Verdouris appeared to lose his temper. He got up and circled around to Jack's right.

"You sit there and say, 'No, I didn't do this,' " Verdouris told Jack, his voice rising. "Yes, you did! Your wife's dead. It's time to be a man, to own up to it. Your father never did that. So, can you?

"Act sensible," Verdouris continued. "The only way to help yourself now is to be honest with us. If you loved them."

"That's something your father never did for you," Cranford told Jack.

"Have the balls to be a man like your father never was," Verdouris said.

Jack drew back inside himself, and Cranford knew he was slipping away. She wished that Verdouris had stayed down. *I almost had him*, she thought. *But here comes that mask again.*

"I'm going to tell you something, though, Jack," Cranford said. "We will be seeing you again. And I'm sorry that your father taught you so well."

"He didn't teach me anything about what you're talking about," Jack said.

Both detectives stood up. So did Jack. They gave him their business cards. As she handed her card to Jack, Cranford tried one last zinger.

"Your dad was around long enough, Jack, to teach you not to be man enough to accept these things," Cranford said.

"I'm going to tell you something, Jack. We're not going to go away," Verdouris said.

"And I'll tell you something too, okay?" Cranford added. "I would much rather that you come to me and say I need help, than for me to have to come back here and hunt you down, or wherever you go. Because there's nowhere you can go, Jack."

The interview was over.

Thirty-eight

Two days later, the story of the Barrons and Roberta Butler finally broke into the public eye—just as Garza and Cranford had suggested to Jack that it would. It thus appears that the authorities elected to leak the fact of their investigation to put pressure on Jack.

In a front-page article in the *Times-Herald* of Vallejo, staff writer Richard Freedman chronicled the deaths of Irene, Jeremy, Ashley, and then Roberta.

"Authorities inexplicably ignored the tragic pattern when Jack Barron's 34-year-old wife, 4-year-old son and 4-year-old daughter—all presumed healthy—died suddenly," Freedman wrote. "But the shocking Feb. 27 death of Barron's mother—52-year-old Roberta Ann Butler of Benicia—did not elude the local police department."

Freedman interviewed Lt. Mortensen of the Benicia Police Department, who confirmed that an investigation was underway and that Jack had been interviewed. Mortensen would neither confirm nor deny that Jack was a suspect.

Two days later, the twice-weekly *Benicia Herald* picked up the story, saying the local police department considered Roberta's death to be a potential homicide, but that the Solano County Coroner's Office had not yet determined the cause of Roberta's death.

That wasn't true, of course; the autopsy report by Solano's Dr. Peterson citing "asphyxia due to smothering" had been signed on March 3, more than a month earlier. But investigators wanted to keep Jack guessing, it appears, and so withheld the cause.

Thereafter, over the next two months, the *Benicia Herald* reporters tracked down a number of Roberta's friends for interviews, including Bea Kennedy. Most of Roberta's Safeway colleagues were quoted, many remarking that Roberta's death seemed suspicious to them.

Following their interview with Jack, the Barron task force sat down to review the videotape, with an eye toward evaluating Jack's responses.

The thing that struck Garza most was Jack's apparent placidity when confronted with the assertions that authorities believed he had killed Roberta and Irene. To Garza, there was no real emotion in Jack's denials—certainly not the level of emotion one might expect from a man wrongly accused.

Certainly, Garza thought, an innocent man would first be horrified at the information the investigators had presented—that Roberta had been smothered to death—and would then demand to know what the police were doing to catch the killer. And once an innocent man learned that police suspected *him*, an innocent man would do one of two things: he would fervently deny it and express repeated outrage, or he would say that the police were completely wrong, and refuse to answer any more questions without consulting a lawyer. But Jack did neither.

To Cranford, the solution to Jack's otherwise inexplicable behavior seemed clear enough: Jack loved being the center of attention, and in the interview, all the attention was focused on Jack. The plan had almost worked; on at least one occasion, or perhaps more, Cranford thought Jack was on the verge of spilling his guts, but something always made him draw back.

Cranford also began to form an idea of what made Jack tick. She began to believe that Jack had killed his family, not because of Elmore, but because he loved it when people felt sorry for him.

Meanwhile, back in Sacramento, Dr. Reiber of the Coroner's Office was going over Irene's autopsy one more time. Although the detectives in their interrogation had told Jack that they knew he had smothered Irene, Reiber hadn't come to that conclusion yet, at least officially.

While he knew of Peterson's findings in Solano County about Roberta, Reiber deliberately did not want to read Peterson's autopsy report out of concern it might bias him. But Reiber already had his suspicions; as he said later, once he had heard of Roberta's death, he was sure there was no natural or toxic cause of Irene, Jeremy, and Ashley's deaths, because there were no commonalities other than Jack.

By late March of 1995, the long-ignored photographs from Irene's autopsy had finally been developed. Now Reiber sat down with the photographs, along with the paperwork from Schmunk's earlier report, and tried to figure out whether there was evidence of Irene being smothered.

Reiber now paid close attention to the photographs of the bruises on Irene's body, particularly the markings on her right biceps, calf, and foot. Coupled with the way Irene's arms had been positioned—left arm extended past the right shoulder, right arm down by her side—these could be evidence of what had happened: that someone, holding a pillow over Irene's face to seal off her mouth and nose, had used a left knee to hold down her right arm, thus causing the biceps bruise. The bruises on the calf and foot, Reiber theorized, might have occurred as Irene struggled to free herself from the weight over her face; Reiber visualized Irene's right leg and foot banging violently against the wooden side of the waterbed as she fought to free herself.

As for Irene's neck, the photographs showed significant

hemorrhaging in the neck area—findings consistent with compression of the neck by some outside force.

Finally, the photographs showed small, red, semi-circular indentations behind Irene's right ear. These, Reiber thought, were probably the result of fingernail markings left by the assailant as he held the pillow tightly over Irene's face for a lengthy period of time.

All of which raised the question about the pillowcase—the one with black streaks of apparent mascara, the covering of the possible murder weapon. Would there be evidence on the pillowcase, such as hair, saliva, or fingerprints? Could the pillowcase be linked to Jack? The pillowcase had been taken by the Coroner's Office when Irene's body was removed to the Coroner's. Where was it now?

A check of the records was made, but the pillowcase could not be found. Neither the Coroner's Office, the crime lab, nor the Sheriff's Department knew what had become of it. Either it had been thrown away, or returned to Jack Barron, more than two years before.

Thirty-nine

Cranford went to visit Starla Hayes. Starla looked back on her few months with Jack with mixed emotions. On one hand, she liked Jack; on the other, it was clear they could never live together.

Jack simply didn't deal with children very well, Starla told Cranford.

Cranford asked Starla to tell her about the night that Irene died.

Jack had come to work that night, Starla said, looking pale and sick. When she'd asked what was wrong, Jack told her that he was worried about Irene. Irene had been having bad headaches, Jack told Starla; he hadn't wanted to come to work, but Irene insisted because they needed the money.

Sounds like Jack is already working on his alibi, Cranford thought; later, if asked, Starla could say that Jack had told her that Irene was sick even before he left, Cranford reasoned.

On that night, Starla continued, she'd gotten sick herself, and Jack had driven her to the hospital in her Chevrolet Suburban. They had arrived around 3 A.M., and Starla was in treatment for nearly three hours. Cranford asked Starla whether Jack had been at the hospital the whole time, but Starla couldn't say for sure.

So, Cranford thought, *Jack could have left the hospital while Starla was being treated, driven home, killed Irene, and then returned in time for Starla to be discharged.*

She and Jack had left the hospital around 6 A.M., Starla said, and Jack had driven her home. He then left, Starla said.

That left the question of what Jack was doing from about 7 A.M. to 9:30 A.M., when he'd finally driven up to the house on Southbreeze. It did not appear that Jack had returned to work to finish his shift. Cranford wondered whether Jack simply drove around, aimlessly, waiting for Christina Hamilton to find Irene's body.

During her interview with Starla, Cranford formed the belief that Jack and Starla had begun an affair before Irene had died; whether this belief was the result of Starla's information, or because of stories told to Cranford by Denise Call, and Jack and Starla's co-workers, isn't clear. Later, Cranford was to assert in legal papers that Jack did in fact have an affair with Starla before Irene's death, just as Irene had suspected, and that it was his desire to get rid of Irene to make way for Starla that was one motive for Irene's murder.

However, still later, Starla was to contend that there had been no affair, prior to Irene's death; that she hadn't moved into the Southbreeze house until about a month after Irene was gone, and that even then, there was no sexual relationship between Jack and Starla until more time passed.

But the relationship didn't work out, Starla told Cranford, because of Jack's rigid habits and his difficulty in dealing with children.

Like how? Cranford asked.

Like when he told his son that Jeremy would go to where

his mommy was if he didn't shut up, Starla said, and as Starla told the story of Jeremy slamming his head against the wall, crying for his mommy, and Jack's angry outburst, Cranford's blood ran cold.

A few days after seeing Starla, Cranford traveled to Pilot Hill to interview Jack and Norma Paget. It was the first time anyone from the Sheriff's Department had come to see them since Irene had died.

Cranford at first contented herself with trying to find out the Pagets' perceptions of how Jack and Irene got along. The senior Pagets said it appeared to them that Jack and Irene got along well, and that Jack was a normal and loving father. It was only after Irene, Jeremy, and Ashley were gone that doubts began to set in. As time went by, Jack and Norma began to believe that things hadn't been as all right as they seemed; that Irene had been having trouble with Jack but had never told them about it.

Why do you say that? Cranford asked.

Because, said Jack and Norma, we found this.

The Pagets handed Cranford a letter written by Irene. It had been, they said, in the box of Irene's things that Roberta had boxed up and given to them—the same box they'd put in the pump house after *Ashley's* death. It was only when two of Norma's sisters visited that spring that they'd looked inside.

Cranford took the letter. It was in Irene's handwriting, and it was addressed to her husband, Jack Barron.

I am really sorry you're unhappy right now, Irene wrote. *... We usually have so much fun together. We have so much to be happy and thankful for ... It really upsets me when I hear you talk about divorce ... Things have been so good for us for so long, you don't just wake up one day and suddenly decide something like that.*

The letter went on about other matters, and then was signed, *All my love, Irene.*

Wow, Cranford thought. *I guess it wasn't as lovey-dovey as Jack wants us to think it was.* And another thought occurred: *Too bad we didn't have this letter when we were grilling Jack.*

Forty

As April neared its end, John Paget remained in contact with Cranford. By now he knew of Roberta's death, even though Jack had never told him about it.

Cranford told John about the five-and-a-half-hour interrogation, and that she, at least, believed that Jack had come near to confessing. She thought that if someone in the family could talk to Jack, could confront him, that Jack might get mad and say something incriminating.

As it happened, Jack had been calling John for several weeks, but John refused to take Jack's telephone calls. John assumed Jack wanted him to do his income tax again, but John wouldn't have any part of it.

"Here it was around the end of April," John recalled, "and it was early April when he made the first contact. Since I hadn't contacted him, he's starting to get worried about his tax return getting done. So I think he's probably thinking, 'Well, John will probably put me on an extension.' But he decides to call in early April and find out when he should send the stuff and so forth. When I got the call, I told my secretary I don't want to take this call. I don't want to talk to this man.

"Then he called again, a follow-up call. So I called

Maryl Lee, and I said, 'Jack's calling about his fucking tax return. What am I supposed to do?'

"That's when she had just finished the interrogation. And she says, 'Well, I'd like you to call him back, if you can.' And she says, 'Get in his face, and try to get a confession out of him.' And she wanted me to record the call."

John was reluctant, mostly because by now he had a strong dislike of Jack, to put it mildly.

"But on the other hand," John recalled, "I wanted to help any way I could to get this guy in jail. So I agreed to call him, and I did. I didn't have recording devices. I went down to Radio Shack, and I bought a tape recorder for the telephone, but it didn't work. I'd tried it out before I made the call, and found out it wasn't working. So I didn't have any confidence it would work. But time was of the essence. She [Cranford] wanted me to do this right away. So I had my secretary get on the telephone with me, because I had no idea of what I was going to say. This was all extemporaneous, off-the-cuff."

John's secretary, listening in, noted all of John's remarks, but not Jack's. Immediately after the call, John went back and tried to reconstruct Jack's portion of the conversation. He later sent the results to Cranford.

The call began with John calling Jack back. Jack answered the phone at Roberta's condo.

"Hello," he said.

"Is this Jack Barron?" John asked.

"Yes."

"This is John Paget. How are you?"

"Fine," Jack said. "How are you?"

John felt his anger well up almost immediately.

"I'm upset with you because you call me about your fucking tax return and you don't even call me to notify me that your mother has died?"

"Well, I've had a lot of things to deal with on this end," Jack said. "But I did have a reason for not calling you."

"I'd love to hear it," John told him.

"Well, we've all been through a lot, you know," Jack said. "And I wanted to spare everyone grief."

"You thought you'd spare grief?"

"Yeah," said Jack, "it's really been tough to deal with everything that's happened, and I'm trying to keep from falling apart."

John could hardly believe his ears.

"Oh, you don't want to start falling apart?" he shouted at Jack. "Well, you fell apart when you killed Irene, you son of a bitch."

"John, I didn't do it," Jack said.

"I don't believe you."

"I swear to you," Jack said, "I didn't do it."

"Four deaths in two years? You don't act like you've lost your family, you don't act like a man who's innocent. Can you prove that you've been following up the deaths? What is wrong with you?"

"I don't know what to do," Jack said. "Everything has been so bizarre. I have been talking to the authorities, but they never tell me anything, and I know Mom called them quite a bit."

Jack kept back the fact that the authorities had just told him they believed he killed Roberta, Irene, Jeremy, and Ashley. But John wasn't to be put off.

"Why?" he demanded. "I want to know why you killed the closest people in your life. Who was an enemy to Irene, Jeremy, to Ashley, and your mom? Who hated them so much as to kill them?"

"I wish I could answer those questions," Jack said, "but it wasn't me."

"It doesn't appear to me or any of our family that anyone else is involved," John told him. "People just don't die."

"I know there's been a lot of innuendo lately . . ." Jack began.

"Innuendo! If you are innocent, why aren't you angry as hell?" John was boiling over.

"I'm just getting extremely tired of all the fingerpointing," Jack said.

"You're extremely tired of it?"

"Well, I just mean that I'm trying to deal with everything."

"You aren't dealing with it," John told him. "People want to know what's going on. You have those answers."

"No, I don't."

"You know, if I lost all those loved ones, the last thing on my mind would be my tax return."

"I've just been trying to take care of business," Jack said. "You know, things still have to be taken care of."

"I had to find out about your mother's passing from my dad, and he found out from Tim, and you didn't even bother to call Tim."

"I did call Tim," Jack insisted, "and I called my cousin. I asked Nancy to go to her mother's house and tell her in person and not on the phone."

John asked Jack who Nancy was.

"My cousin," Jack said. Nancy had gone to Roberta's sister, Jeanne Dillon, and told her that Roberta was dead. Then Nancy, Jeanne, and Tim had called everyone else, "because I just couldn't handle doing it all," Jack said.

"And two weeks later," said John, "you were so well-composed you call my office about your tax return? It doesn't make any sense to me. Would this make sense to you if your sister and her family had all died? What would *you* be thinking?"

"Yes," said Jack, "I know what you're saying, and it doesn't make sense to me either. It's human nature to be thinking that way."

"Do you have a cause of death from the Coroner's Office about how your mom died?" John demanded. "How many times have you called the Benicia Police Department or the Coroner's Office? Do you demand answers?"

"Yes," Jack said. "They said it was suffocation. About

four or five times. They won't tell me anything. They just say they're continuing to investigate.''

''And what do they do?''

''I don't know what they do,'' Jack said. ''It's very confusing.''

''If she suffocated, how and by whom? What do you think?''

''I don't know, but it wasn't me, I swear,'' Jack said. ''Everyone wants to think I did it, but I didn't.''

''It's natural to speculate,'' John said. ''Here is this woman and she suffocates and you were the only one to see her preceding her death.''

''I saw her the night before,'' Jack said, ''because I told her to unplug her phone, because I was expecting a call about work.''

Here was yet another explanation of what happened at Roberta's condo that night. First, Solano County Deputy Coroner Loveless recorded in his notes that Jack had last had contact with Roberta about 10 P.M., ''over the telephone''; then there was Jack's statement to Benicia Detective Monty Castillo that he had actually seen Roberta when she returned from work about 10:15 to 10:20 P.M., and that he'd gotten up around midnight to go to the bathroom, and to make a call *to* his job; and now there was this assertion, in which Jack claimed that he'd told his mother to unplug her telephone so she wouldn't be disturbed in case Jack's job called *him*.

''What time was this?'' John demanded.

''About 10:15,'' Jack said. ''I remember glancing at the clock.''

''P.M.?''

''Yes, P.M.''

''What time do you go to work?''

''About 5:30.''

''What time did the Coroner's Office say she died?''

''I don't know,'' Jack said. ''They won't tell me anything. But I got home about 2:30 and that's when everything kind of transpired.''

''What transpired? What do you mean, everything happened? Is that when you killed her?''

''No, John,'' Jack said. ''I didn't kill her. Why would I do that? She was the only one who was ever there for me. After Irene and the kids died, everyone else just kind of stopped calling.''

''That's why it's so incredible,'' John said. ''Jack, I and the rest of the family were there for you—until it became absurd to be in the same camp anymore.''

''Well, yeah,'' Jack said, ''I can kind of understand how you might have felt, but I don't know . . .''

''Neither do I,'' said John. ''I still don't understand why you aren't leading the charge! I would be so damn mad at the world I couldn't see straight.''

Jack told John that it seemed to him that John had backed away from him, not he from John.

''That's baloney,'' John said. He reminded Jack that he'd invited Jack and the kids to be with his family on Thanksgiving after Irene died, but Jack didn't want to do it. Besides, John said, the family had sent Jack money for the kids.

''You reach a point,'' John said, ''where all the evidence points to you.''

''I was working on Thanksgiving,'' Jack said.

''How long do you think you can go on living like this?'' John asked. ''With all this on your conscience?''

''I don't have a problem with my conscience because I didn't do anything,'' Jack said. ''But things have been tough on this end.''

''Did you see the article in the paper, Jack?'' John asked.

''Yes, I've heard about them, and I saw one,'' Jack said.

''It's in the papers all over California, and probably all over the country,'' John said. ''And you think I'm out of line thinking this way?''

"Well," Jack said, "I can kind of understand how people might be suspicious."

"I found out things after Irene died that neither of you confided in me," John said. "You and Irene were having marital problems. Did you argue the night she died?"

"No, no, John!"

"It's interesting to me," John added, "that in all three cases, after each one died, you said they had a little cold, and they were taking cold medication. Maybe they all just died of colds!"

"You're being awfully cynical," Jack said.

"I don't know why I'd be cynical after . . ."

"Yeah, but I didn't kill Irene."

"You know what keeps coming to my mind? How many men there are in Death Row who say, 'I didn't do it.' Murderers never admit to killing. All I can say is, Jack, God help you."

Jack said he'd been hurting.

"Well, when it comes to being hurt you aren't alone," John told him. "And if you did this, and I think you did, you're the cause of this hurt."

"I didn't cause anyone to be hurt," Jack said. "I'm hurting as much as anyone else."

"Under the circumstances," John said, "I can't help you with your tax return. I'll send your stuff back."

Jack seemed irritated at this news.

"Well," he said, "I wish you could have told me sooner, so I could have done something else."

Now John got mad again.

"We know how important this is, that taxes are done! If I lost my wife, I wouldn't give a damn about business. You are unique in the way you can handle this."

Jack said nothing. John wasn't quite finished.

"Don't come near me or my family," he said. "It better not happen."

"Well," Jack said, "that probably won't happen."

"See you in court," John said, and hung up.

Forty-one

One week later, on May 8, 1995, Dr. Reiber wrote an addendum to the Irene Barron autopsy report of June 8, 1992.

"Since the death of Irene Barron on or about June 8, 1992, there have been subsequent deaths in the family, namely of the two children, Jeremy (date of death 2/7/93, age 4) and Ashley (date of death 8/7/94, age 4) and of Irene Barron's mother-in-law, Roberta Ann Butler (date of death 2/27/95, age 52). These circumstances led to a more critical evaluation of the initial autopsy and scene findings related to the death of Irene Barron."

After briefly describing the circumstances of Irene's discovery, Reiber moved to the heart of the matter.

"Review of the initial autopsy finding," he wrote, "reveals a number of significant findings which were not given a clear initial interpretation."

Reiber now listed eight separate areas of injury to Irene that had been noted in Dr. Schmunk's original report, including the apparent scratches behind the right ear, as well as evidence of injuries to Irene's neck.

"Review of the autopsy photographs confirms the presence of the above-listed findings, and reveals several additional findings not initially listed."

Among these new observations, Reiber reported, were a small abrasion on the left side of Irene's neck, a small bruise on the back of her right shoulder, a bruise on the back of her left leg, a small cut on inside of the upper right lip, and a small bruise inside the lower right lip.

These observations, Reiber said later, were consistent with injuries imparted by Irene's teeth to her own lips, as might be expected if her mouth and nose were forcibly obstructed.

"In summary," Reiber concluded, "a revisitation of the autopsy and scene findings . . . indicates a very high likelihood of an unnatural death by means of traumatic asphyxia.

"The undersigned recommends a revision of the cause of death as given below."

Then, under cause of death, Reiber wrote: "Probable traumatic asphyxia."

At last, nearly three years after Christina Hamilton found Irene Barron lying supine on her marital bed, feet on the floor, with a pillow over her face, the Sacramento Sheriff's Department finally had what they had long demanded: a homicide.

At the end of May, the Barron case again broke into the public prints, this time in the *San Francisco Chronicle*. In a May 30, 1995 page one story headlined "*One Family's 3-Year Tragedy*," staff writer Allen Mathews reprised the events of the previous three years, and said a task force of Solano and Sacramento County officials was looking at all four deaths. Mathews said the task force planned to meet that day to consider its next move and quoted Benicia's Mortensen as saying that the task force members were hoping for some sort of decision.

"We hope we'll have some good news," Mortensen told *The Chronicle*.

The story went on to point the finger at Jack as the prime suspect, although both Mortensen and a representative de-

clined to confirm that Jack was the person they were looking at.

Mathews attempted to contact Jack for his reaction but
failed. He did, however, contact Daniel Russo, whom Mathews identified as Jack's attorney. Clearly, sometime between his grilling on April 17 and May 30, Jack had
realized his legal jeopardy.

Russo dismissed the suspicion that Jack was responsible
for the deaths. "There's no evidence of wrongdoing,"
Russo told Mathews.

Mathews then traced the recent history of Jack and his
family, ending up with a former Barron neighbor on Southbreeze he identified as Diann Tice.

"On Southbreeze Drive," Mathews wrote, "little remains to mark the tragedy that befell the Barron family,
except for the three saplings that Barron planted after each
death."

Mathews drew an evocative quote from Tice.

"There's Ashley, there's Jeremy, and there's Irene,"
Tice said, as she pointed to the trees.

Even if he wouldn't talk to the reporters, the publicity soon
attached itself to Jack as if it were some sort of black cloud.
His co-workers at Amtrak could hardly be expected not to
notice Jack's sudden notoriety.

Once, when Jack got involved in a dispute with a conductor and said the conductor was "an asshole," the conductor came right back at him.

"I'd rather be an asshole than a serial murderer," the
conductor said.

Forty-two

Ever since Reiber had amended Irene's autopsy report, the Sacramento District Attorney's Office had been evaluating the case against Jack Barron. The major difficulty was the lack of strong and direct evidence—like an eyewitness, or some sort of physical evidence that made it clear that Jack, and only Jack, could have committed the crimes.

In fact, from one perspective, even the idea that crimes had been committed might be called into question by a competent defense lawyer. Schmunk's original autopsy report on Irene could be used to counter Reiber's addendum, leading to the possibility of reasonable doubt that a murder had even been committed, if the case ever came to trial. As for Jeremy and Ashley, there was virtually no physical evidence that homicide had taken place.

True, there were unequivocal findings that Roberta had been murdered; but the trouble for the Sacramento authorities was that crime had taken place in another jurisdiction, Solano County. That meant the Sacramento District Attorney's Office had no venue to arrest Jack for Roberta's death.

All of the evidence against Jack was entirely circumstantial. From this perspective it was only Jack who had the motive, the opportunity, and access to the means to commit the crimes, as demonstrated by the witness accounts and Jack's own statements of his actions before and after the deaths.

By far the most important piece of circumstantial evidence was the sheer number of deaths. That four people, all intimately connected to Jack, should die in remarkably similar circumstances pointed the finger of blame directly at Jack.

Despite decades of television actors who claim, on screen, that the evidence against them is "only" circumstantial, and therefore weak, the fact is that the law requires that circumstantial evidence be given the same weight as any other evidence, even direct evidence. Circumstantial evidence may be interpreted by a jury as any reasonable person might interpret facts, along with inferences rising from the circumstances. It is up to the defense to rebut a prosecutor's interpretation of circumstance with an alternative and equally plausible interpretation of the same facts.

Because the deaths of Irene and Roberta were in many ways quite similar—both had been found with injuries suggestive of death by smothering, both had been alive the night before, both had been found in locked dwellings— the death of Roberta helped to bolster the evidence that Jack had also killed Irene.

But because Roberta's death had occurred in Solano County, prosecutors in Sacramento County were not permitted by law to charge Jack with her death in their county. That did not mean that the evidence from Roberta's death could not be presented to a jury in Sacramento, however. Prosecutors in Sacramento believed they could present the evidence surrounding Roberta's death against Jack under the rules of evidence that allowed presentation of facts that demonstrated aspects of character; in effect, Roberta's death could be used to try to prove Jack's guilt in the deaths of Irene, Jeremy, and Ashley as evidence of a "common scheme or plan."

In other words, the circumstances of Roberta's death closely paralleled the circumstances of Irene's death; and the deaths of both Irene and Roberta made it more likely that Jack had also caused the deaths of Jeremy and Ashley as part of the "common scheme or plan."

In the case of all four, the prosecution could argue that Jack's motive was to obtain the life insurance proceeds; and it might also be possible to argue that Jack's scheme to get the proceeds was carried out, in all four cases, by the act of smothering each victim under very similar circumstances.

Besides the number of deaths and the possible common scheme involved in each, the prosecutors had one other apparent commonality: that it was only Jack who in each case had access to the victim. Crucial to this was the development of the various timeliness: the evidence indicating that Irene had died before Jack left the house, and that no one had presumably entered until Christina Hamilton; that Jack was alone with the children prior to Jennifer Walters' arrival and subsequent discovery of Jeremy; that Jack was alone with Ashley prior to Jill Presley's arrival, and that he might have had an opportunity to enter the house while Jill was asleep; and that Jack was alone with Roberta from 10:15 P.M. to the time he left for work at 5:30 A.M.

All these circumstances combined made it appear that of all the people in the world, only Jack could have been in the right place, at the right time, with a possible motive, and with the means to do his own family to death.

But before charges could be brought, the questions of jurisdiction and precedence had to be worked out with Solano County.

On May 30, 1995, these issues were addressed by the Barron task force. And while Solano County might have a prior claim on Jack, in that the Benicia police were the first to investigate and the Solano Coroner was the first to find death by homicide, the Barron affair was a bit more complicated than that.

Solano County Deputy District Attorney Chris Pedersen, who attended the May 30 meeting, later recalled his argument to both counties: if Jack went to trial in Solano County for Roberta's murder, the worst penalty he might expect to receive was 24 years to life. But if Jack were tried by the Sacramento authorities—and convicted—he might face the death penalty.

And, if Jack were convicted of multiple murder in Sacramento, that in turn would allow Solano County to later try Jack for special circumstances—having been tried and convicted of multiple murder—and *also* ask for the death penalty; in effect, by lying back until Sacramento finished with Jack, it was possible for Solano County to hit Jack with a second death penalty sentence, thereby making sure that between the two counties, one or the other might make him pay the ultimate price for the deaths of his wife, children, and mother.

As a result of the May 30 discussion, and subsequent meetings, it was decided that Sacramento would take the first crack at Jack.

Later, Solano's Pedersen recalled the situation—despite the fact that Castillo and Garza had worked as hard as they had to get evidence against Jack as the murderer of Roberta, they agreed with the strategy of allowing the Sacramento authorities the first chance.

There was very little of the traditional rivalry between police agencies that one might expect, Deputy District Attorney Pedersen later recalled.

"We had no glory hogs," he said. "What we had was the slug of slugs, and everyone wanted to make sure he was put away."

Forty-three

By Monday, July 17, 1995, on what would have been Irene Barron's thirty-eighth birthday, Cranford and Verdouris obtained an arrest warrant for Jack. They called their colleagues in Benicia and said they were on the way. The Benicia police put Roberta's condo under surveillance, in case Jack got the sudden urge to bolt.

Just before noon, Cranford and Verdouris arrived at the Benicia Police Station, at the town's City Hall complex just a bit south of Military Road. Then the two Sacramento detectives drove toward Jack's house.

Just about 12 P.M., Jack exited Roberta's condominium, got in his van, and drove down the hill toward the Southampton shopping center. He pulled up near a supermarket, and was flagged down by a Benicia patrol unit.

Cranford and Verdouris advanced on Jack.

"Mr. Barron, you're under arrest for the murder of Irene Barron, Jeremy Barron, and Ashley Barron," Cranford told him, and Verdouris pulled Jack's hands behind his back and cuffed him.

All the way to Sacramento, Jack said nothing. He sat in the back seat of the detectives' car and said not a word, even when he was booked into the Sacramento County Jail and held without bail.

*   *   *

John Paget was sitting in his Fallbrook office when someone from the Sacramento County District Attorney's Office called him with the news of Jack's arrest.

John's immediate reaction was one of relief.

"This had been building for so long," he recalled later, "and so much had happened, it seemed like it was taking forever to reach a point where they finally felt they could arrest him." Finding out that his former brother-in-law was in custody was deeply satisfying—especially since the arrest had come on Irene's birthday. It was, somehow, a bit like Irene striking back.

John soon got on the phone with Jack and Norma, Debra Harris, and Denise Call to spread the news.

With Jack's arrest, publicity about the Barron case exploded.

In *"Man Arrested in String of Family Deaths,"* the *Sacramento Bee* brought the previous contention between the Sacramento Coroner's Office and Sheriff's Department into the open for the first time.

"Even law enforcement officials concede that the case was mishandled from the beginning," wrote *Bee* reporters Sam Stanton and Dan McGrath.

The Sheriff's Department tried to put a positive spin on the situation. A spokesman for the department claimed that the Sheriff's detectives "were on the case all along, that veteran child abuse and homicide detectives were working on it, and that meetings among detectives, the District Attorney's Office and the Coroner were held regularly to discuss the case." However, the spokesman didn't say that most of this activity didn't start until after Roberta had died.

The Pagets' reaction was reported, as was that of Jeanne Dillon, Roberta's sister.

"This is great news," Jack Paget told the *Bee*. "We've been waiting for it for a long time. We feel it should have happened a long time ago."

"Oh, my God, they've done it!" exclaimed Jeanne, in an interview with the *San Francisco Chronicle*. "We've been waiting for this for so long, maybe now justice can be done."

From Shasta, Dave and Patty Bednarczyk weighed in on Jack's side.

"He's been a very big part of our lives . . . part of the family, really," Patty told the *Bee*. "If I believed he was capable of something like this, I never would have allowed him in my home, with access to my kids. But the Jack Barron we know is not capable of this. If there's another Jack Barron that we don't know, we've never seen any sort of behavior to make us wonder."

"If Jack's guilty, he needs to admit it and take his punishment," Dave said. "It's a matter of accountability. I just don't happen to believe it. You wouldn't be human if you didn't wonder, and I asked him over and over. I wanted him to tell me the truth. He'd look me in the eye and say, 'Dave, I had nothing to do with those deaths.' I never got the feeling he was lying or being evasive. All I'm interested in is the truth. If it turns out Jack's guilty, I'll still stand by him. I may hate what he did, but I'll love him regardless."

Amidst all the publicity, there was yet another voice heard from: Elmore Barron. The *Bee* tracked Jack's father down in the southeastern United States and asked him for his reaction.

"It bothers me, and if he did in fact do all of this I'd like to be the one who pulls the switch at San Quentin on him, because if I brought this turkey into the world I want to be the one who takes him out," Elmore told *Bee* reporter Sam Stanton.

Stanton interviewed Cranford, who told him of the investigators' suspicions that Jack had killed his family because of his unsatisfying relationship with Elmore.

"He hated his father," Cranford told Stanton. "His father had abandoned the family when Jack was very young, and every time Jack behaved irresponsibly, his mother would complain that he was acting like his father.

"His father was born on Sunday, August 7, 1938," Cranford continued. "Ashley was killed on Sunday, August 7, 1994. Jeremy and Irene died on Sunday the seventh as well, Jeremy in January of 1993, Irene in June of 1992. I don't know what the explanation is, but it's more than co-incidence, and I'm sure it's tied to the father."

In his interview with Stanton, Elmore disputed Cranford's characterization of his divorce from Roberta as "abandonment," but halfway agreed with Cranford about Sundays the seventh being a motive.

"It sounds to me that he knew I was going to hear about this sooner or later—the seventh," Elmore told Stanton, "and he knew it would ring a bell with me. And I don't know if he was jealous because it was sometimes such a big to-do over my birthday than his."

When he left Roberta, Elmore said, Jack was 12. Elmore said he'd given Jack a choice of which parent to live with, and Jack had chosen Roberta.

Over the next 20 years, Elmore told Stanton, he'd seen Jack only about three times, and talked to him on only a few occasions.

Elmore sounded as though he didn't like Jack very much.

"I worked for the Southern Pacific railroad for 30 years," Elmore said, "and he's a railroad buff, and every time I get around him, that's all he wanted to do, was talk trains, and it just irritated me. I could stand to be around him for like a day."

Forty-four

Justice may be done, as Jeanne Dillon hoped, but to be well done, if often takes a long time.

More than six months after Jack's arrest, he remained in the Sacramento County Jail, waiting for a preliminary hearing to decide whether there was enough evidence to warrant a trial on the charges that he killed Irene, Jeremy, and Ashley.

Part of that delay had been occasioned by Jack's changing of attorneys. Daniel Russo, who had originally been retained by Jack, had to drop out. Because Jack was for all practical purposes a pauper, his case was assigned to the Sacramento County Public Defender's Office.

On February 1, 1996, a preliminary hearing before a district court magistrate, Rudolph R. Loncke, was begun to determine whether there was sufficient evidence to hold Jack for trial in the Superior Court. The hearing was to last for parts of four days. It would be up to Loncke to decide whether the case should be sent to the Superior Court for trial. There was only one witness, an investigator attached to the District Attorney's Office, Tricia Hacker.

It had been Hacker's job over the preceding months to read every report and witness statement filed in the Barron case by the two Coroner's offices, the Sacramento Sheriff's Department, two different fire departments, the Benicia Police, and the Barron family's personal medical histories. After this, Hacker contacted each witness named in each report or statement in an attempt to verify the accuracy of the information that had been written down. In some cases, Hacker had conducted new interviews, including a face-to-face meeting with Dr. Schmunk to discuss his inconclusive autopsies of Irene and Jeremy.

Now in the preliminary hearing, Hacker would be questioned by Assistant District Attorney John O'Mara in an effort to present evidence that murder had been committed in Sacramento County, and that it had been done by Jack Barron.

O'Mara was 49, and so highly regarded as a specialist in prosecuting homicides that he had earned the nickname "Mr. Murder" in Sacramento. His own boss, the elected Sacramento County District Attorney Jan Scully, once called him the "guru of homicide prosecutors."

"He's got great insight into judges, he understands people, and juries, he can read cases as far as their viability for prosecution and he has a work ethic beyond compare," Scully told the *Sacramento Bee*.

In this preliminary hearing, O'Mara's task was fairly straightforward: he had to present, through his questions and Hacker's answers, enough facts to show that murder had been committed, and that there was probable cause to believe that only Jack could have been the murderer. Because Hacker would be the only witness, O'Mara would have the opportunity to go through his entire case before Jack's lawyer would have a chance to cross-examine.

Demonstrating that murder had occurred was the first major hurdle, particularly since Dr. Schmunk had first determined that he could not ascertain the cause of Irene's death. If Jack had a first line of defense, it would lie in Schmunk's inconclusive findings, which if anything were far more consistent with murder than those from the autopsies of Jeremy and Ashley. O'Mara's objective was to establish that Schmunk hadn't *ruled out* the possibility that Irene had been suffocated.

O'Mara began by having Hacker describe the events of the discovery of Irene's body, taking care, through her testimony, to establish that the house had been securely locked the morning Irene was discovered. He followed with the arrival of the paramedics, then Schmunk and the Coroner's deputy, taking particular care to establish that Schmunk had taken Irene's liver temperature at the scene.

O'Mara introduced a number of photographs taken at the scene, including several that showed the relationship between Irene's body and the pillows.

"Now," said O'Mara, "you also had occasion, did you not, to review an autopsy report as well as a scene report prepared by a Dr. Gregory Schmunk; is that correct?"

"That's correct," said Hacker.

"And you had the opportunity recently to meet with Dr. Schmunk in person; is that correct?"

"Yes," Hacker said.

After O'Mara asked about Schmunk's qualifications as a pathologist, he turned to Schmunk's findings. Hacker testified about Schmunk's discovery of the various petechial hemorrhages and bruises, and the small cuts behind Irene's right ear.

"What significance, if any, did he describe for you the finding of those phenomena, petechial hemorrhage, and the other hemorrhage you've described?" O'Mara asked.

"[He] stated it could be associated with asphyxial death," Hacker replied.

After taking Hacker through the rest of Irene's autopsy results, O'Mara asked if Schmunk had ever determined a cause of death for Irene.

"He arrived at a cause of death as undetermined," Hacker said.

"Did you discuss that with him in your face-to-face meeting here in January this year?"

"Yes, I did," Hacker said.

"Was he able to describe for you—although he could not single out a specific mechanism that caused her death—was he able to single out the kinds of things that could cause her death that he would be unable to detect at autopsy?"

"Yes."

"And what category or categories did he delineate to you for that regard?"

"Some naturally occurring disease process that would leave no evidence—at autopsy, or some toxicological substance that, you know, was undetected, some strange chemical that was undetected; or an asphyxial death."

After a few questions about methods of asphyxia designed to show that the most likely cause of Irene's death was smothering, O'Mara turned to Dr. Reiber's addendum.

"And when [Reiber] reviewed the autopsy of Irene Barron the second time," O'Mara asked, "he had occasion to request that the photographs taken by Dr. Schmunk be printed so that he personally could view those; is that correct?"

"That's correct."

"What, if anything, did Dr. Reiber tell you that he found out as a result of the second review of the autopsy of Irene Barron?"

"He stated that the photographs of Irene clearly depicted the injuries already noted in Dr. Schmunk's report but they also highlighted injuries not previously mentioned," Hacker said.

After questions and answers detailing the additional injuries noted by Dr. Reiber in his addendum, O'Mara asked if Reiber had formed any conclusion as to the cause of Irene's death.

"That the cause of death was probable traumatic asphyxia."

"Did Dr. Reiber come to the conclusion . . . based upon one finding, or, how did he arrive at that process, could you tell us? Did he describe that process for you?"

"Yes, he did," Hacker said. "He described it as an additive interpretation of the autopsy findings on Irene. He said her findings did not correlate with death caused by cardiac arrhythmia and cardiac deaths.

"Reiber has not seen the spectrum of injuries that were apparent in Irene's case," Hacker added. "And there were no structural abnormalities in her heart."

Now O'Mara had presented evidence that Irene had been murdered; next he had to show that it was probable that Jack had been home when the death occurred.

The hearing continued, with O'Mara taking Hacker through Jack's reported movements on the night Irene died, including Jack's trip to the hospital with Starla Hayes. What O'Mara was attempting to show was that Jack, if he hadn't suffocated Irene before leaving for work, had a second opportunity after taking Starla to the hospital.

"Did she indicate whether or not Mr. Barron was present, to her knowledge, in the hospital with her while she was receiving treatment?"

"She wasn't certain," Hacker said.

"Did Starla Hayes make any comments to you during her interview as to conversations that she had with Mr. Barron the night that his wife died, relative to his wife?"

"Yes, she did."

"What did she say in that regard?"

"She stated when he came into the store that night he looked—he looked sick and he looked pale. She asked him what was wrong and he stated he had a really weird feeling about leaving Irene that night because she was having a lot of headaches. He had asked her if she wanted him to stay home. She told him she didn't want him to lose the pay."

The implication was that Jack was already preparing the

ground, with Starla, for the idea that Irene was sick, possibly fatally so.

Next, O'Mara established that Jack had received $15,000 in life insurance proceeds following the death of Irene. This testimony would be used to provide the glue necessary to bring in evidence later relating to Roberta's death, even though that case was the responsibility of another jurisdiction.

Over the next day, O'Mara would present evidence relating to the deaths of Jeremy and Ashley, primarily the autopsy findings that disclosed there was nothing wrong with either child prior to their deaths, and the statements of Jennifer Walters and Jill Presley about Jack's actions before, during, and after the discovery of each.

As for Jeremy, O'Mara had Hacker relate Starla's recounting of Jack's remark to Jeremy about going to where his mother was as an indication of Jack's state of mind toward his son.

Through his questions to Hacker, O'Mara suggested that Jill had simply been wrong when she told the police that she'd checked Ashley about midnight; or, perhaps, he said, she might have been feeling guilty about falling asleep, and so asserted a check that hadn't actually been made. Or, alternatively, Jack might have slipped away from work, driven across town, and smothered Ashley as Jill slept.

In this way, O'Mara was able to demonstrate that it was possible each child had been suffocated, and that it was possible for Jack to have done it, either before the arrival of Jennifer Walters, as with Jeremy, or before or after the arrival of Jill, in the case of Ashley. In both cases, O'Mara demonstrated that Jack had received insurance settlements of more than $13,000.

This set the stage for evidence related to Roberta's death. This time, of course, the pathology findings were unequivocal, since Solano County's Dr. Brian Peterson had determined that Roberta had been smothered to death.

O'Mara concentrated once again on Jack's movements before, during, and after Roberta's death. In questions to Hacker, O'Mara demonstrated that the house was locked when Jack left to go to work, and it was still locked when he returned.

Again, as in the Irene and Ashley situations, O'Mara attempted to demonstrate that Jack had at least two opportunities to commit murder; in the case of Roberta, Jessica Vasquez' observation of Jack at 12:30 P.M. could be evidence that Jack had lied about his whereabouts during the day.

The observations of Roberta's neighbor Margaret Hawes were testified to, including the fact that the blinds had not been opened. Tim O'Keefe's evidence about Jack's cryptic observation at the restaurant—that Roberta and Irene looked alike in death—was brought out, as were Carol Marino's observations of the tension between Roberta and Jack in the days before Roberta's death.

Finally, O'Mara demonstrated that Jack stood to receive nearly $130,000 in life insurance on his mother once she was dead: another piece of evidence of the "common scheme or plan" that linked all four deaths to Jack.

With all the evidence in, it now fell to Jack's lawyer, Assistant Public Defender Don Manning, to poke as many holes as he could in O'Mara's case.

Manning was 52, an Air Force veteran, and a colonel in the Air Force reserve. He had been trying capital cases in Sacramento for more than a decade, including one notorious serial murder case in which a man and his wife had together victimized ten women at random.

Manning knew the strongest evidence implicating Jack was the sheer number of deaths. But Manning believed that if he could show that it was doubtful that any of the Barrons had been murdered, and that it was possible Roberta had died during a time when it could be proven that Jack was at work, the case against Jack would collapse.

Manning's strategy was to attack the inconsistencies in O'Mara's case—the equivocal autopsy findings on Irene, the absence of clear causes of death for Jeremy and Ashley, along with support for the assertion by Jill Presley that she had seen Ashley in a different position than the one she was later found in, at a time when Jack was presumably at work.

As for the death of Roberta, Manning would seize on Dr. Peterson's wide aperture for the time of death, and suggest that, not only was Jessica Vasquez completely wrong about seeing Jack at 12:30 P.M., it was possible that Roberta had died after Jack had left the condo at 5:30.

To demonstrate these points, Manning had to chip away at Hacker, thereby suggesting that the District Attorney's Office was so intent on prosecuting Jack that it overlooked obvious holes in the case against him.

Manning began with Irene's death, and asked Hacker whether she had discussed Schmunk's statements to the Sheriff's Department's original detectives, Lauther and Riesdorph, with Schmunk himself.

"So," said Manning, "you then did not discuss Detective Riesdorph's conclusion, after talking to Dr. Schmunk—you did not discuss those conclusions with Dr. Schmunk?"

"No, I did not," Hacker said.

"For instance," said Manning, "there is a page [in Riesdorph's report] that says, 'Dr. Schmunk concluded that a cause of death could not be determined at this time. He stated that toxicology and tissue examination may help decide the cause of death. Dr. Schmunk could not rule out suffocation. However, he stated that the absence of bruising or petechia in the lips was a factor against smothering. Do you recall that?"

Hacker said she knew about Schmunk's original statement to Riesdorph, but didn't discuss it with Schmunk when she interviewed him in January of 1996.

The import of this was the notion that at the earliest stages, Schmunk had told the detectives that smothering wasn't very likely in Irene's death, and that Hacker hadn't pursued this angle in her interview with Schmunk. This was one way of trying to suggest that there was no real evidence that Irene had been smothered, and that therefore, Jack was not responsible for her death.

Manning pressed the issue. Had Hacker reviewed Schmunk's autopsy report on Irene? And hadn't Schmunk indicated in his report that there was "no evidence of trauma and cause of death undetermined following complete autopsy including postmortem toxicology and cervical cultures?"

"That's correct," Hacker replied.

"And in discussing the case with Dr. Schmunk in 1996, did he indicate to you that his conclusion would be the same, that the cause of death is undetermined in the case of Irene Barron's death?"

"Yes, he did," said Hacker. "But he agreed with Dr. Reiber's report also."

"But he said he would not change his report, is that right?"

"I don't specifically recall asking that question, no," said Hacker. "But I did review with him Dr. Reiber's amendment and he said he agreed with that and felt comfortable with that."

"Now, Dr. Reiber's addendum report was prepared in May of 1995, is that correct?" Manning asked. Manning was trying to set up the argument that Reiber had only produced his addendum after Roberta's death had been attributed to smothering by Solano County authorities, and that it was therefore biased.

Hacker agreed that Reiber had made his addendum in May of 1995, more than two months after Roberta's death.

"The bottom line is," said Manning, "after discussion with Dr. Schmunk in January of this year, 1996, Dr. Schmunk did not say, 'Wait a minute, let me change my autopsy report from 1992, I want to give a different cause of death.'"

"No," said Hacker, "he did not state that."

Having now tried to establish that the cause of Irene's death was still a matter that even the experts might disagree on, Manning moved toward the other apparent holes in the case against Jack. He turned to the pillowcase with the apparent eye makeup that had been noted by Schmunk in his scene report—the pillowcase that had somehow disappeared.

"Is there anything in this file that suggests that any analysis of any pillowcase was done," Manning asked Hacker, "that suggests that this so-called mark on the case was in fact makeup?"

"No," said Hacker, "there was not."

"Have you researched to determine whether or not either the Coroner's Office, the Sheriff's Department, the Sacramento crime lab, or any law enforcement agency, has, in effect, that pillowcase in its possession today?"

"Yes," said Hacker.

"And what are your conclusions?"

"That we've been unable to locate the pillowcase," Hacker admitted.

On the following Monday, the preliminary hearing resumed, with Manning still working to establish the notion that homicide by suffocation had never been definitively established by the Sacramento authorities.

Hacker admitted that in the cases of Jeremy and Ashley, there had been no finding that suffocation was the cause of death. She insisted, however, that Reiber had not been able to rule out murder in Ashley's case.

That prompted Manning to zero in on the inconsistencies of time and motion in the Ashley situation. Hadn't Jill Presley told everyone who would listen that she'd observed Ashley in bed around midnight, and had seen her a second time, in a different position, around 4 A.M.?

"In fact," said Manning, "in your conversations with the baby-sitter in Ashley Barron's case, the baby-sitter indicated to you that Ashley Barron was on her side with the sheet covering at least a portion of her body when she first observed Ashley, is that correct?''

"That's correct," said Hacker.

"And you indicated that the baby-sitter informed you that she had observed Ashley around midnight?"

"She said shortly before midnight."

Manning now asked whether Hacker had reviewed Cranford's interview with Jill, in which Jill had said that she'd checked Ashley twice before finding her dead at 4 A.M. Had Hacker seen Cranford's report?

"Yes," Hacker said.

"Did she confirm that she had in fact checked Ashley twice before the final check?"

"No, she did not," Hacker said. "She was somewhat confused about how many times she checked Ashley and at what times she did check her."

Manning thus attempted to demonstrate that it wasn't clear that Ashley hadn't been alive after Jack left for work. In other questions, Manning demonstrated that it would have been impossible for Jack to leave work for an extended period of time in the early morning hours without someone having noticed he was gone—especially since Jack had been in charge of the shelf-stocking on the night Ashley died.

Next, Manning tried to show that Jack might not have been present when Roberta died, primarily by focusing on Dr. Peterson's imprecision as to the time of her death.

"Now," said Manning, "when you talked to Dr. Peterson about the time of death, as you did with the other doctors, what did he inform you was the time of death in this case?"

"He stated that it could be minutes before the 911 call to hours before," said Hacker.

"All right," said Manning. "But in your report, didn't he specifically state . . . [that] based on the degree of lividity present and the early onset of rigor mortis in the extremities he would estimate the death to have occurred definitely less than 12 hours and possibly less than six?''

''That's correct,'' Hacker said.

In fact, Manning pressed, hadn't Dr. Peterson suggested that Roberta died less than six hours before Jack found her body?

''That's correct,'' said Hacker. ''He stated there was no positive way to determine the time of death, other than witness information.''

If Roberta had died only six hours before the discovery—around 8 A.M.—then Jack could not have killed her, since he was on his way to work at 5:30 A.M., Manning's question implied.

Now it was O'Mara's turn again. His objective was to plug up the holes Manning's questions had exposed.

As for Jill Presley's state of mind during her interviews, O'Mara tried to show that Jill was upset and so might have been confused as to the time she first checked on Ashley.

''And in fact, she was so despondent at one point after the death of Ashley, I believe in November of the same year that she died, she, Miss Presley, tried to commit suicide, isn't that correct?''

''That's correct,'' said Hacker.

As for the time of death, O'Mara said, wasn't it true that the criminalist, James Beede, had determined from the undigested stomach contents that Ashley had been suffocated shortly after eating dinner?

''That's correct,'' Hacker said.

And hadn't Dr. Reiber estimated the time of death of Ashley Barron? O'Mara asked.

''Dr. Reiber, yes.''

''And what did Dr. Reiber say?''

''Four to six hours,'' Hacker said.

''I don't have any other questions, Your Honor,'' O'Mara said.

Forty-five

The following day, both sides returned to court for their final arguments. It would be O'Mara's job to tie all the circumstances together, and to convince Judge Loncke that there was probable cause to believe that murder had been committed and that Jack was the culprit. Manning, on the other hand, would have to demonstrate that it was not clear that murder had taken place in any of the Barron cases, and that in two of the cases, there was evidence that Jack was elsewhere when the deaths occurred.

After some preliminary remarks in which he suggested that the circumstances of Irene's death strongly suggested that Jack was to blame, O'Mara reached the meat of his argument.

"Now," he said, "I suspect that Mr. Manning will say, 'Well, you know, people die suddenly and unexpectedly every day. You can pick up the newspaper every day and see that happening.'

"We might say that that might happen in an isolated instance, but I want you to view these cases in the context in which all four occur."

O'Mara continued:

"Certainly people in isolated instances die unexpectedly,

even people that are in arguably very good health. We read about basketball players or other persons who are at least on the surface . . . in excellent health, at a chronological age where they're not predisposed to dying suddenly, yet they die.''

But in the cases of all three Barrons, there was absolutely no medical or toxicological reason for their deaths, O'Mara continued. As for Roberta Butler, it was apparent on examination of the evidence that she had been murdered the night before her body was found.

"So," he said, "we have four deaths within a family in the space of less than three years. And even genetics don't explain this. I mean, there's no genetic line you can follow all the way through this. There's no relationship between the victims no matter how you look at it."

Except one, O'Mara went on to say.

"All of the decedents were in some way related to Jack Barron. All died in their bed. All were in some form of bed clothing. All were last seen by Jack Barron. All bear the same non-specific kinds of findings, although in the case of Roberta Butler the pathologist was able to come to a cause of death.

"Just to sum up," O'Mara concluded, "in my view the appropriate way to view [this] case is to view all four of the homicides together. There is no explanation for four deaths in one family in this short a period of time, where three of the deaths have no logical medical reason to explain their occurrence. It just defies logic. It defies any kind of analysis one could proffer."

That was all wrong, Manning said when it was his turn.

"The District Attorney has to suggest that you look at the four [deaths] together, because if you looked at each of these cases individually there would be no evidence of any criminal act whatsoever," Manning said.

"So the District Attorney suggests that, gee, let's lump all of these together. And what are the odds—he doesn't use that term, but that's basically what he's suggesting to the court—what are the odds that four members of one person's family could have died in a three-year period? Don't look at the fact that we can't tell you what caused their deaths. Just look at the fact that in fact four people died over a three-year period, and what are the odds? It must be a criminal act.

"And," Manning continued, "I don't believe that the District Attorney has established in any fashion that clearly in the cases in Sacramento that there was any criminal act here."

The judge questioned Manning about Jack's reported remark to Jeremy, about sending him to where his mother was.

"I was going to address that," Manning said. "We all get agitated. We're tired, we're agitated, the child is acting out, the child is throwing a fit, a tantrum, and such that, we all say things we don't mean to say.

"Every one of us at some point has said something to a loved one we regret," Manning continued. "And if there's one parent who hasn't said one thing to a child that he regrets the entire time he has raised that child, I don't think there's one where that hasn't happened."

Manning summed up his position.

"It's our contention," he said, "that the deaths here were naturally caused deaths. That we can't explain it. The doctors can't explain it. We can't explain it either. But there are many unexpected sudden deaths that are caused by a disease that does not manifest itself during autopsy.

"The District Attorney has not come in here and said—he has not brought one person in here to suggest that Jack Barron said anything to his wife or to anybody that, I don't want to be married to this woman anymore, I hate this woman, I'm going to kill this woman.

"He has had nothing. There's been no testimony whatsoever concerning that. There has been no testimony whatsoever concerning anything other than his love for his wife and his love for his children. You have no evidence whatsoever of anything to connect Mr. Barron to the unfortunate deaths of his family members other than suspicion and speculation.

"And," Manning concluded, "that suspicion does not rise to the level of probable cause to believe that a crime was committed nor probable cause to believe that Mr. Barron was the instrument of those deaths."

The judge asked O'Mara if he had anything else to say.

O'Mara did. For a man who loved his wife so much, O'Mara said, and was supposedly concerned about her health, it was curious that Jack had never once called Irene on the night she died to see if she was all right. And it was even more curious that, within a month of her death, that same loving husband had taken a new partner.

Judge Loncke took no time to deliberate with himself before issuing his decision.

"I think," he said, "the evidence before the court, which includes a pattern of death over three years, where Mr. Barron was the last one to see each person, and all the other evidence before me, leads to my strong suspicion that the charged crimes were committed, and that Mr. Barron is guilty thereof."

Jack would be held for trial.

Epilogue

Three years later, and almost six years after the death of Irene Barron, Jack Barron was still in the Sacramento County Jail awaiting his trial. With Jack's very life hanging in the balance, justice moved very slowly indeed.

What was the truth? Had Jack Barron methodically murdered his whole family, one by one, smothering each with a pillow as they lay in bed? And if he did, why? Despite all the speculation, all the conjectures, all the armchair psychology, any possible motive seemed as mysterious as the deaths themselves.

For his part, Jack, through his lawyer, Manning, continued to insist that he had done nothing—that in fact, his was a tragic case of almost unbelievable circumstance, a repository of the unfathomable fates that took first his wife, then his children, then his mother, and then his liberty, and possibly even his life.

But the slowness of justice should not obscure some of the more ominous questions remaining from the Barron case.

Among those is the most painful: if Jack indeed had suffocated Irene, was the apparent laxity by Sacramento authorities indirectly the cause of three other deaths? Would

Jeremy, Ashley, and Roberta Butler be alive today if the Sheriff's Department had acted sooner to investigate the circumstances surrounding Irene's death?

What about the autopsy photographs that were never developed—the photos that convinced Reiber, two months after Roberta Butler died, that Irene had been murdered almost three years earlier?

What about the friction between the Sheriff's Department and the Coroner's Office, the lack of coordination and communication that allowed the deaths of all three Barrons to go uninvestigated for so long?

For the Paget family, at least, the answers to all those questions are clear: the system failed, and three people died needlessly because of that failure. And even if Jack Barron is eventually convicted of the crimes, there is nothing that will ever be able to ease that family's pain.

"An entire family," Jack Paget said, "has been wiped out."

SHE LOVED HER SONS...TO DEATH.

Hush Little Babies

THE TRUE STORY OF A MOTHER WHO MURDERED HER CHILDREN

DON DAVIS

Not since the Susan Smith case has a murder so shocked the nation: a beautiful, loving mother is horrified to find her two young sons stabbed to death on her living room floor by an intruder. Hearts go out to poor Darlie Routier, who appeared to live for her children. But overwhelming evidence soon finds Darlie, the neighborhood's "Most Wonderful Mom," guilty of slaying her own innocent children in cold blood...

HE STOLE THEIR HEARTS—THEN TOOK THEIR LIVES...

SMOOTH OPERATOR

THE TRUE STORY OF SEDUCTIVE SERIAL KILLER GLEN ROGERS

Clifford L. Linedecker

Strikingly handsome Glen Rogers used his dangerous charms to lure women into the night—and on a cruel date with destiny. For when he got them alone, Rogers would turn from a sweet-talking Romeo into a psychopathic killer, murdering four innocent women during a six-week killing spree that would land him on the FBI's "Ten Most Wanted" list. Finally, after a twenty-mile high speed police chase, authorities caught the man now known as one of history's most notorious serial killers.

SMOOTH OPERATOR
Clifford L. Linedecker
___96400-5 $5.99 U.S./$7.99 CAN.